Dua Lipa

Dua Lipa

THE UNAUTHORIZED BIOGRAPHY
Caroline Sullivan

Michael O'Mara Books Limited

First published in Great Britain in 2023 by
Michael O'Mara Books Limited
9 Lion Yard
Tremadoc Road
London SW4 7NQ

A CIP catalogue record for this book is available from the British Library.

This product is made of material from well-managed, FSC®-certified forests
and other controlled sources. The manufacturing processes conform to the
environmental regulations of the country of origin.

ISBN: 978-1-78929-484-2 in hardback print format
ISBN: 978-1-78929-486-6 in trade paperback format
ISBN: 978-1-78929-485-9 in ebook format

1 2 3 4 5 6 7 8 9 10

Front cover image credit: dpa picture alliance / Alamy Stock Photo
Back cover image credit: Michael Hickey / Getty Images
Cover design by Ana Bjezancevic
Designed and typeset by Design23
Printed and bound by CPI Group (UK) Ltd, Croydon, CR0 4YY

www.mombooks.com

CONTENTS

Chapter 1

BIG POP GIRL

When Dua Lipa walked on stage at the AO Arena in Manchester on 15 April 2022, she did so as the world's biggest pop star. It was the first British show of her thrice-postponed Future Nostalgia tour, and there she was: tall, radiant, powerful. At the sight of her, encased in a neon-pink Balenciaga catsuit and full-length gloves, the cheer from 21,000 fans rattled the rafters. This was the first time she had played a full live show in her home country in more than three years, and she was the very picture of pop majesty. Not to over-egg things, but this was a coronation.

From that moment, Lipa's place on the pop throne was assured. The reviews that appeared after the show bristled with superlatives: 'An all-killer set,' said NME; 'Dua Lipa is a superstar,' agreed the *Daily Mail*; and the *Guardian* made do with 'A huge star she undoubtedly is, complete with an arena full of fans going nuts at whatever she does.'

Tour statistics corroborate that: on the first leg, for instance, before the twelve UK/Ireland dates, she grossed $40 million for twenty-nine shows in North America. The reaction there had been as frenetic as it was at home: when she played New York's Madison Square Garden on 1 March, to cite one example, the floor shook. Actually shook. 'Everyone just kind of rode the wave with me,' she told Jimmy Fallon a few days later on *The Tonight Show*. *Billboard* magazine helpfully noted that $40 million was an increase of 346 per cent over the proceeds of her last US tour in 2017–18 and predicted that the whole ninety-one gig outing, which also visited Europe, South America and Australasia, could earn $100 million.

To use a different metric, *Future Nostalgia* and Lipa's self-titled debut album are among the most streamed albums by a woman on Spotify, and Lipa was also the first female artist to amass over 1 billion Spotify streams for each of five songs ('IDGAF', 'New Rules', 'Don't Start Now', 'One Kiss' [with Calvin Harris] and 'Levitating' [with DaBaby]). Alternatively, we can judge her stature by a uniquely British method: she's now famous enough for newspapers to take an interest in her finances. In March 2022, the *Daily Mail* ran a story about her two companies, Dua Lipa Live LLP and Dua Lipa Limited, being worth a total of £51.6 million. Unlike the many artists who had a pretty thin time of it during the coronavirus pandemic, Lipa actually became £5.5 million better off between 2020 and 2022, thanks to ticket sales for the tour. It had been announced at the end of 2019, and tickets continued to sell through the two years of lockdowns as concerts were postponed, rescheduled and more added. It says something that nearly all fans opted to hold on to their tickets rather than ask for refunds.

A few weeks after that *Mail* story, another headline in the same paper: 'Ed Sheeran and Dua Lipa cash in from Amazon warehouse workers: Pop stars rake in millions from music played in background at "industrial premises".' What it boiled down to was that in 2021 Sheeran's hit 'Bad Habits' and Lipa's 'Levitating' were the two most played songs in workplaces like warehouses. The royalty distribution body PRS for Music reported that it had collected £18 million for tunes played over the PA systems at such places (not just Amazon's warehouses but any industrial place of work that did this). That £18 million didn't go straight to Lipa and Sheeran, however; it was split between dozens of acts whose music was also played. So, the image painted by the headline – that Lipa had earned a fortune by the sweat of Amazon workers' brows – was misleading. That she's done well for herself in the past seven years is not in question – those websites that estimate the wealth of famous people reckon that her personal worth in 2022 was $36 million, while *Heat* magazine's Richest Celebrities Under 30 list put it at £69 million the same year – but 'rake in' is unnecessarily sensational.

Anyway, raw numbers say nothing about how she got to this point or why people who were at the AO Arena show practically melted social media afterward. 'Oh my FUCK,' one fan wrote zestily in the Popjustice forum. 'Dua Lipa is incredible and she had every single person in Manchester under her spell. Levitate me, Queen!' Another listed the elements that made the gig worth waiting two years for: 'Wow what a: show / superstar / crowd / set list / outfits / choreo / vocals / production. I was so blown away by everything tonight.'

A third admirer mused meaningfully, 'Mmmm, this imperial phase.' Coined by Pet Shop Boy Neil Tennant, 'imperial phase' denotes the remarkable moment in an artist's career when everything goes right: creativity is at its peak, critical acclaim floods in and the public can't seem to buy and stream enough of their work. Along with all that, Lipa's imperial phase has been saluted by four waxworks, on display at Madame Tussaud's Museums in London, Amsterdam, Sydney and New York.

On the other hand, you could just take the BBC's word for it. Music correspondent Mark Savage's review was headed, 'Dua Lipa's Future Nostalgia tour confirms she's Britain's best pop star'. Then there was the opinion of Dua herself. Facing the AO Arena audience, she simply said, 'This is the best welcome home ever.'

It must have felt that way. The tour was originally slated to take place in the spring of 2020. When that was called off because of the Covid pandemic, the dates were shifted to early 2021, then autumn 2021, both of which also became untenable. The tour finally got the all-clear early in 2022, by which time fans had been waiting two years to see a show based around an album that itself was two years old. (The *Future Nostalgia* LP was released on

27 March 2020 – four days after the Prime Minister announced stringent restrictions on British public life.)

What couldn't have been foreseen was the degree to which Lipa's career would accelerate during the enforced lay-off. Though she was already successful, as witnessed by the size of the venues booked for the gigs – where previously she had mainly played theatres, *Future Nostalgia* took her into the arena class – the time off saw her star ascend dramatically. In late 2020, looking back at a transitional year for the singer, her then manager Ben Mawson said, 'Dua is the No. 1 star in the world.' Taking into account that he was her manager and was duty bound to say that, he wasn't wrong. Though 2020 was a bit early to proclaim global dominance, the gist was correct: if she wasn't yet the world's No. 1, she soon would be. Obviously, it wouldn't have happened if Lipa hadn't been endowed with abundant songwriting nous and a sultry, coiling mezzo-soprano voice (to really appreciate how good she is, check YouTube for clips of her singing acoustically). Yet it would be wrong to think that luck hadn't also played a part. She is an adept creator of stone-cold bangers, the kind of songs that prompt a rush to the dance floor every time they are played. But who could have known that this new cluster of anthems, packaged as an album with the suddenly apposite title *Future Nostalgia*, would appear the exact week Britain was told a 'new normal' was now in effect?

That's where she got lucky: the savviest promotional strategist couldn't have picked a better time. Nor could they have guessed that people would develop a strong bond with the record as lockdown wore on. It wasn't the only new pop album on the block

— Charli XCX, Lady Gaga and The Weeknd also released at roughly the same time — but by virtue of its bass-driven upfulness it was the one that most resonated. *FN* became the soundtrack to staying at home, a joyous constant that withstood repeated listening and made it possible to imagine a time when real life would resume.

Like everyone else, Lipa spent lockdown working from home, but she was a constant in her own right, tirelessly promoting the record on TV and in the press. She kept her social media updated, sometimes livestreaming from her kitchen. She was openly emotional in her streams, compassionate toward those who were suffering but also optimistic. You could imagine having her as a friend — a friend who was better-looking and more gifted than yourself, perhaps, but one who also had a compensating sense of humour and was as down to earth as they came. Combined with the fizzy delight that was *Future Nostalgia*, she was unassailable.

A snippet from a 2016 interview with British journalist Peter Robinson is a particularly enjoyable example of her ability to see the ridiculous side. Speaking to her shortly after she was longlisted for the BBC Sound of 2016 award (it was won by songwriter Jack Garratt), he remarked that Lipa had benefited from tastemaker support — being written about and played by the 'right' people. Consequently, she was viewed as highly cool. But what if, Robinson suggested, she wasn't cool at all? What if, in fact, her CV was full of what tastemakers would see as unforgiveable uncoolness?

'Imagine if I described a pop star to you,' said Robinson. Imagine if before landing a record deal, that pop star had had a surprisingly unhip past. What if she'd gone to the Sylvia Young

Theatre School, whose alumni included soap stars and boy-band members? What if she'd sung in a TV ad for the 2013 series of the cheesiest reality show of all time, the *X Factor* (though she didn't compete in the show)? Furthermore, this same pop star had had a brief career as a model. A model! Nothing riles music purists more than models who reckon pop stardom is the next step, as if being beautiful weren't enough. This pop star Robinson was describing had had a very brief modelling career, however, because she wasn't small enough, and was pushed by her agency to 'lose a lot of weight'.

So, picture this pop star and all these impediments to true coolness ... 'And yet I still somehow managed to stay cool,' crowed Lipa. 'Maybe it's just me – maybe I'm just really fucking cool.' It's hard not to love a pop singer so keenly aware that coolness is in itself a ludicrous construct. She's also just plain funny. On the subject of tour merchandise, she'd already given it some thought: 'I do want my own personal hot sauce.' She embodies the adage, 'almost anyone can be a pop star, but not everyone can be a witty pop star'.

Accordingly, when the UK moved to Step 4 of the 'roadmap' out of restrictions in July 2021, Lipa had cemented her place as the pop star who had made the album that saw the country through hard times.

Having said that, it wasn't just luck that set the wheels in motion. Fate also had something to do with it. The last few years – an aeon in pop terms – had been dominated by R&B and by sadgirl, a label invented to describe music by Billie Eilish, Lorde, Phoebe

Bridgers and their downtempo ilk. It encouraged brooding and introspection, and in the age before social media might have been only a niche genre. But because sadgirl (a patronizing name that trivialized music made and listened to by women) existed in the time of Instagram and TikTok, it spilled over into the wider consciousness and became commercially popular. Note that it was underpinned by some of the best singles of recent times – credit is due to Eilish's 'Bad Guy', Lorde's 'Royals' and many more.

There was nothing remotely downtempo about *Future Nostalgia*, or about Lipa. The album was thirty-seven minutes of endorphin-raising dance-pop with hooklines that embedded themselves in the memory on first listen. That decidedly didn't equate to thirty-seven minutes of shallowness, though. Lipa's vocals, purposeful and committed, showed her belief in the songs – and the songs were fantastic. Their emotional catchment area was wide: there was the giddiness of meeting someone new and luscious ('Hallucinating'), and there was that coming-up-for-air sensation in a new relationship that was so intoxicating she had to ask her partner to help her calm down ('Pretty Please'). But she also wrote about being on the receiving end of toxic masculinity ('Boys Will Be Boys') and the perverse pleasure of sex with someone she couldn't stand in a relationship that was held together by sex alone ('Good in Bed'). And what about that glorious moment when she was finally so over some loser that she could tell him not to waste his time trying to win her back ('Don't Start Now')?

To backtrack to the start of 2020: there was Lipa, about to unveil a new record in which a great deal of money and effort had been invested. That was where fate, or perhaps predetermination, came into it. Pop was due a change in direction, and since early 2018 she'd been assembling an LP that offered exactly that. It was neither sadgirl nor R&B and felt fresh and optimistic. Freshness and optimism were in short supply in early 2020, as Covid inexorably made its way to Europe. *Future Nostalgia* was there, newly minted, to provide it.

Once heard, it demanded to be played again; it was good enough that it could be listened to from end to end with no skipping of tracks. If Lipa could make an album with no duff material or filler, she was among a small coterie of artists at the top of their game – 'the total package', as a fan said. She had evolved in a way that few pop stars do unless they have talent and ferocious drive in equal measure. It was as if all her efforts since the start of her career – the patient honing of songwriting skills, the widespread touring and the unfailingly articulate promotional interviews – had been directed toward this moment.

Chapter 2

BEGINNINGS

When I was growing up all I wanted was to be called Hannah, Sarah, Ella ... anything normal,' Lipa told the *Observer* in April 2018. 'Because with Dua you had to explain: "I'm from Kosovo."' Apparently, she gave serious consideration to changing her name to Amber. But by 2018, she was proud of 'Dua's distinctiveness. (It means 'love' in Albanian; she has no middle name.) With a confidence bestowed by six hit singles (a seventh, 'One Kiss', would soon join them), Lipa had come to see her name and her heritage as points of pride. Not only that, being 'different' was now a full-scale plus in her professional life, because there was only one Dua in the music industry, and she was it.

She was even able to laugh when people mispronounced

it in public. An American talk-show host made a small piece of internet history in 2018 by calling her Dula Peep, inspiring online hilarity and its own entry in the Urban Dictionary. ('Dula Peep is a mispronunciation of famous pop singer's name Dua Lipa, said by Wendy Williams, host of *The Wendy Williams Show*.') With that said, she wasn't even all that exotic. There were other successful musicians of Albanian origin, from fellow Londoner Rita Sahatçiu – better known as Rita Ora – to Americans Bebe Rexha and Ava Max and New York rappers Action Bronson and Gashi. There were family connections, too. Ora's film-director grandfather, Besim Sahatçiu, knew Lipa's historian grandfather, Seit Lipa, in Kosovo – Dua's father posted a picture of Seit and Besim together in a restaurant in the 1960s, from which it can be seen exactly where Dua got her luxuriant eyebrows. Another coincidence: Dua's mother's maiden name was Rexha.

Lipa was born in London but spoke Albanian at home and grew up fully conversant with Kosovo's fraught history. 'My parents have made sure that I never forget the place where I'm from,' she told America's *Nightline* news programme in 2018. Her mother and father, Anesa and Dukagjin (known as Dugi), left Kosovo's capital, Pristina, in 1992, fleeing the Bosnian War and Slobodan Milošević's 'ethnic cleansing' (as had Pristina-born Ora and her family slightly earlier). They were just two of the estimated 1 million Kosovar Albanians who left the country during that period. It was an appalling position for the couple to be in, but the decision to go was taken out of their hands. 'My grandmother on my mum's side is from Bosnia. I think because of that my parents moved [because her ethnicity put them at greater risk]. There was just too much conflict,' Dua told *Line of Best Fit*.

There was also the treatment of Seit Lipa. As head of the Kosovo Institute of History, Seit was ordered by Serbian lawmakers literally to rewrite the history of Kosovo — to state that it had never been part of Yugoslavia but was always part of Serbia. (While relations between Serbia and Kosovo have since been 'normalized', Serbia does not recognize Kosovo as an autonomous country.) He refused and lost his job. Most Albanian schools in Kosovo also closed during this time. A family friend, Florent Boshnjaku, told the *Sun* in 2019 that merely being related to an academic made it too dangerous to stay: 'Every academic was a target.' Some people vanished.

After Anesa and Dugi claimed asylum in Britain and moved into a flat in north-west London, they were unable to return to Pristina to visit Seit. Dugi didn't see his father again before he died of a heart attack in 1999.

In London, there was at least the comfort of being with other Kosovars — a substantial diaspora had settled around Camden, providing a ready-made social circle and source of information. Back home, Anesa (pronounced Ah-NESS-a) had been training as a lawyer and Dugi a dentist. 'Did I *want* to be a dentist?' he mused in a 2018 interview. 'I was studying it because it would provide you with something you could live on [financially].' He was also attracted by the fact that dentists and doctors had status in society — but dentistry wasn't his passion, and it fell by the wayside when he moved to London.

In London, he formed and sang in an Albanian-language rock band called Oda, whose most popular song was 'Beso nëe Diell' ('Believe in the Sun'). It's a soft guitar track, seemingly created for late-night listening; the melody is plaintive, and Dugi's voice cracks with yearning. It works regardless of whether you understand Albanian — the emotion transcends any language barrier. In a westernized comparison, he sounds like a cross between Chris Rea and Hozier.

A recording of 'Beso nëe Diell' found its way to Kosovo and became popular enough to inspire multiple cover versions by other Kosovar groups. One of the best was by his own daughter, who sang it during a show in Pristina in 2016. Dua's aching interpretation shows her in an entirely different light, the pop star replaced by a melancholy torch singer. (She'll be missing a trick if she doesn't make an Albanian-language record at some point.) The star of that night, however, was Dugi, who joined her on stage halfway through the song. The audience had been enthusiastic enough while Dua was singing the tune, with most of the crowd vigorously singing along. But the sight of her father, striding out from behind the band's backline equipment, provoked unfettered joy, with screams erupting, camera phones appearing and a chant of 'Dugi! Dugi!' filling the air. 'Prishtinë!' he replied, and the delight rose another notch. He took over on vocals and his impassioned delivery offered a glimpse of the rock star he must have been.

Dugi had arrived in London with a bit of music-business experience already under his belt, having sung as a teenager in Yugoslavia and had a No. 1 song in the chart there when he was sixteen. After arriving in Britain, he wanted to continue to make music. There was an audience on his doorstep, some of whom would have known of him in Yugoslavia, so there was nothing to lose by forming a band and playing shows. Once they settled on Oda as a name – its Albanian meaning was 'a room in a traditional house where guests gathered to share traditional epic ballads' – and wrote a few songs, they began to get gigs. The response to 'Beso nëe Diell' and the other newly hewn material was enthusiastic enough to warrant making an album.

Recording in a makeshift studio in a friend's bedroom, they pressed a thousand copies, sold the lot and pressed more. Dugi estimated that the final sales tally was 20,000 albums – a decent figure, especially considering it was achieved mainly through word of mouth. Dua credits her early interest in music to having seen Dugi's group, and he corroborates this: wherever Oda played, a toddler Dua was there, watching from backstage. The band split up in 1998.

Twenty years later, Dua would also benefit from the goodwill Dugi and Oda had accrued among Kosovars both in Britain and back home. Her first video, for 'New Love' in 2015, racked up far more views than anyone on her team had expected for an unknown artist. When they checked the figures, it turned out that most were from Kosovo.

An unexpected corollary of Dua's fame has been the tabloid press's interest in her father. It's based entirely on his looks and was initiated by a comment made by comedian Jack Whitehall when he hosted the 2019 Brit Awards. Dugi attended with Dua, who was nominated in four categories and won in one (British Single, 'One Kiss'), and found himself the subject of special attention from Whitehall. Interviewing Dua at her table in the audience, Whitehall asked, 'Do you know how much of a dad-crush I have? Your dad is the coolest dad.' 'This is really getting out of hand,' riposted Dua. Undeterred, Whitehall said, 'This is the silver fox over here – the best-looking dad in the music business!' Dugi, dapper in evening dress and not dissimilar in features to George Clooney, affected an expression halfway between modesty and mortification. His Instagram follower-count rose to 178,000 after the show, and as of this writing has reached 299,000.

Since that night, he's been the subject of regular media coverage, which in one sense is helpful, as it draws attention to the Sunny Hill Festival, the annual Kosovo music event he has staged since 2018. On the other hand, he now has to contend with being of interest to paparazzi when out on private errands. He accompanied his daughter to a house viewing in London in April 2019, and in an article that subsequently appeared in the *Daily Mail* he even made it into the headline ('Dua Lipa … goes house hunting with her "silver fox" dad'). Two of the photos in the article were of Dugi alone.

There's not much he can do about that, or about the pile-on of pop media that discovered him thanks to Jack Whitehall at the Brits and have been a bit giddy ever since. To cite just one example, PopSugar believes he's 'a total babe' who induced 'a full-on swoon fest' at the Brits – not the kind of thing Dua, or anyone, wants to read about her father. She says he takes it all with a pinch of salt, finding it funny and a bit silly. The rest of the family just laughs about it.

His attractiveness, and Anesa's, had embarrassed her for years. At school, she cringed when boys told her that her mother was 'really hot' and girls said Dugi was 'so fit'. She can laugh at it now, but at the time it made her feel different from everyone else when all she wanted was to blend in.

Dugi and Anesa *were* a handsome pair. A photo taken before they left Pristina shows them arm-in-arm in an urban garden, dark-haired and casually dressed. Anesa has her head thrown back and is smiling radiantly; Dukagjin, lips parted, is putting on the full smoulder. When he posted the picture on his Instagram account on Anesa's forty-eighth birthday – 28 June 2020 – he captioned it, 'The time we fell in love.' The couple are a model of stability in a way rarely found today: Dugi was Anesa's first boyfriend, they married young and their long union has been happy and secure. On their silver wedding anniversary, 10 March 2020, Dua paid tribute to 'the strongest love I know' with a picture of them on a beach when they were in their twenties. Both model-beautiful, they sit back on their beach chairs, smiling and resting their hands on each other.

After arriving in London – she was then twenty, he twenty-three – they took bar work at a pub near their flat, the Globe Tavern. (They held their wedding reception, in March 1995, at the Globe.) Dukagjin went to business school at night and Anesa retrained in the tourism sector, both bent on becoming productive and self-sufficient as soon as possible. Dugi would become a marketing specialist. His LinkedIn page lists a number of high-profile jobs, including the post of advertising coordinator for Mean Fiddler PLC, the company behind the Mean Fiddler venues and the Reading and Leeds Festivals. Currently, he's CEO of the Pristina-based Republika Communications, and also CEO of Mercy & Wild, a London-based PR company. Additionally, he's chief innovations advisor at Faraday Future, a Los Angeles tech company that develops electric cars.

Dua, born in August 1995, was aware of her parents' sacrifices as soon as she was old enough to comprehend. Anesa and Dukagjin could talk for hours about their experiences, but at other times found it too depressing to look back. 'They say they feel they've lived through 300 years,' Dua said in November 2021 at a ceremony held by the Atlantic Council, where she received the Washington DC-based think tank's Distinguished Artistic Leadership Award. Her British-Kosovar identity had made her what she was, she added, endowing her with 'an immigrant work ethic'.

'You understand something on a personal level. That no refugee leaves their country without having to,' she told the *Observer* in a 2018 interview. 'I've seen my parents work every day of my life.' Their ability to adapt to their circumstances greatly impressed her, and she took to heart a maxim of Dukagjin's: 'You have to work really, really hard, just to have a tiny bit of luck.'

She inherited their ethic. Years later, Joe Kentish of Warner Records, her label since 2014, said her industriousness is so renowned that he uses her as an example to other artists. He was particularly struck by her appetite for work when, after finishing *Future Nostalgia*, she immediately began to plan Album Three. Most musicians would take a break after an intensive two years' writing and recording, especially in light of the gruelling promotional cycle that would shortly ensue. Not her. Rather than have even the briefest holiday, Lipa was straight into thinking about the next record. (By summer 2022, it was half finished, but she says that she's in no hurry to release it.)

Going back to her early years, she grew up in north-west London and remembers her childhood as happy and secure. There's footage of her as a five-year-old that testifies to that. It's a brief clip, filmed in her living room, presumably by one of her parents. It catches her in the middle of singing along to S Club 7's 2000 hit 'Reach' (aka 'Reach for the Stars') and having a sensational time. Holding the CD booklet, Dua 'reads' the lyric as she sings; what is striking is how comfortable she is in front of the camera. Wearing a white dress with a DKNY logo and pushing her hair out of her face so she can see the lyrics, she puts a good deal of effort into her performance.

It's obvious that she's seen S Club on TV, because she's aware that simply singing the tune won't do. The seven-piece group specialized in chirpy pop creations accompanied by simple dance routines that anyone could follow, so they were an excellent starter band for kids who loved music and movement. Dancing up to the camera, she dramatically casts her eyes heavenward, clutches the booklet to her chest and throws an arm upward. Impressively, she then hurls the booklet over her right shoulder and – Shirley Bassey-style big finish – flings her arms out to the sides. This is a kid in need of a stage. Lying on the sofa behind her, her infant sister Rina seems unmoved, but what does she know? It has to be said that there isn't much to distinguish Dua's voice from that of any other five-year-old, but by nine it had acquired more depth and she was singing in a lower register.

Years later, she was asked whether it was hard to grow up with a father who was passionate about music himself. Did his love of it make it less pleasurable for her – as if singing were 'homework'? Absolutely not, she replied; she had always adored music. When the family were out in the car, she always sang along to whatever CD was playing, especially if it was *The Miseducation of Lauryn Hill* (a favourite of her parents that Dua now considers one of the best albums of all time). If anything, being reared in a musical household sealed her fate: she knew from the start that she wanted to perform, and her parents had no say in it. When the Lipas had friends over, Dua would persuade their children to sing and dance with her, and the adults would be informed that all conversation would have to stop because the kids were about to put on a show. In the school playground, she organized dance routines to songs she loved, often by Nelly Furtado or P!nk. A career in performing, therefore, was almost inevitable.

Furtado and P!nk were formidable influences on Dua. The first album she was ever given was Furtado's 2000 debut *Whoa, Nelly!* and she received P!nk's 13 million-copy-selling second LP *Missundaztood* soon after its 2001 release. Both impressed her to an extent she hadn't thought possible. She was too young to really know anything about either artist, other than that they seemed cool and exciting and she wanted to be exactly like them. It wasn't an outlandish ambition. Canadian singer-songwriter Furtado, whose Portuguese parents named her Nelly Kim so she wouldn't have an 'ethnic' name at school, and Pennsylvania-born P!nk were relatable, as far as pop stars went. Both prioritized artistry over glamour or sexiness, made addictive pop singles and looked like they were having a roaringly good time doing it. Dua was floored by, as she told Glamcult in 2016, their 'bad-bitch attitude'—not the phrase she would have used as a child, but by 2016 she saw their independence as formidable and inspirational. Stylistically, they were relatively easy to emulate, too. While few ten-year-olds of the era could realistically look like Britney Spears—cropped tops, luxuriant mane and all—Furtado and P!nk were casual, T-shirted types who could be copied with a single visit to Topshop. And style was important to Dua, even at that age. A picture from the early 2000s shows an already-brewing appreciation for fashion: her shaggy pink jacket, geometric-print blue top and dark jeans aren't simply a set of clothes thrown on by an active six-year-old; they're an Outfit, with a capital 'O'. It's easy to imagine her wearing them now, modishly clashing colours and all.

What's harder to imagine is her doing it with a shaved head. She says she was born with unusually fine hair, and when she was six her parents decided that shaving it off entirely would stimulate thicker growth. 'I was rocking a bald head!' she told Digital Spy, with the kind of insouciance it's only possible to muster years after the event. Her mother advised her to deflect criticism by saying she'd modelled herself on Demi Moore's character in *G.I. Jane*, and Anesa's faith was justified. When it grew back, her hair had the silken lustrousness of a shampoo-ad model's.

Her early education took place at Fitzjohn's Primary in Hampstead, an Ofsted-rated 'good' school, where Melanie Blatt of All Saints was a former pupil. In its 2002 report, when Dua was seven, Ofsted noted that 15 per cent of pupils were refugees, 'mainly from Kosovo'. The report also said that high attainment in music was one of Fitzjohn's strong suits and made an observation that's intriguing in this context. Lipa has said that she auditioned for the school choir when she was nine but was unsuccessful because she was asked to sing a high note that she couldn't reach. The teacher told her to try again the following year, the implication being that she wasn't good enough. Ofsted, on the other hand, approvingly recorded the fact that every junior pupil was in the choir: 'No one is excluded.' It's important to recognize that choir rules might have changed between the 2002 inspection and Lipa's 2004 audition, which would explain the apparent disparity between the Ofsted report and her own experience.

The rejection was enough of a knock that Dua almost dropped the idea of ever singing to anyone other than family. (In 2020, with two smash albums behind her, she began to work with her vocal coach to broaden her range so she could hit higher notes.) Her parents weren't having that. They knew she could sing well and that giving up would be a waste. So what about going to theatre school? It was their idea, but once Dua enrolled in Saturday classes at the Sylvia Young Theatre School in Central London, she loved it.

She was noticed by an instructor, who saw potential and put her in a class with fourteen-year-olds. She had to sing in front of them — an appalling prospect for a nine-year-old, especially one who was physically small — but once she got up there and the older kids didn't laugh, she began thinking of her ability as something she could harness.

Singing wasn't just about being able to hit notes, she came to believe; it was a confidence booster and a route to self-belief. The teacher's most valuable advice during Dua's two years there was probably: 'Don't let anyone tell you what you can or can't do.' Recalling it during a 2019 interview with *Wylde* magazine, Lipa was still grateful: 'That really helped me; it opened my eyes. I was really young and didn't have to listen to anyone else if I believed in myself.'

By age twelve, living in Pristina and enrolled at the Mileniumi i Tretë School, Dua indisputably could sing, high notes or not. Her performance in a school contest called Kosovo's Got Talent revealed a voice that was coming into its own: low, full-bodied and true. Alicia Keys herself couldn't have faulted Dua's take on her 2007 chart-topper 'No One'. The audience even gave her a spontaneous round of applause halfway through.

Back in London, however, she never got into the highest group at Sylvia Young because it was a theatre school, with the emphasis on 'theatre'. Most of the students were following a musical-theatre path, and Lipa later counted herself lucky that she didn't make it to the top. It would have imprinted Broadway mannerisms onto her singing style and even, God forbid, left an unconquerable desire to use jazz hands in her delivery. She did, however, discover the value of teamwork and 'always helping someone up', she told Complex in September 2016. (Her interview with the magazine had been arranged to promote her debut album, scheduled for release that month. At the last minute, because Lipa felt it needed extra work, the date was pushed back to February 2017; then, in order to accommodate 'some new songs and exciting collaborations', it was changed again to June 2017.)

Fitzjohn's, or its playground, was also the site of an important life lesson. The playground game kiss chase was popular with the younger boys, who chased the girls and kissed them if they caught them. Seven-year-old Dua went along with it for a while but found it stressful. She knew that being chased was a 'compliment', but detested it for that reason — why should she try to win a boy's approval, or pretend she even liked the idea of being kissed? Unfortunately for the boys, she discovered a technique that unmistakeably conveyed her feelings. When one chased her, she would beckon him closer, and pinch him in the delicate spot between neck and shoulder until he literally fell to his knees. The boy wouldn't try it again, and Dua could congratulate herself on standing up to him. Asserting herself fed into her embryonic feminism. Even at that age, though she probably couldn't have articulated it, she was anti-patriarchal; revenge-pinching was a form of justice, as far as she was concerned.

At Fitzjohn's, having been pushed by her parents to learn an instrument, she took up the cello. Their suggestion had been guitar or piano, but she was drawn to the cello in what she later thought of as a rebellious act. She was a small kid, and it was the largest instrument she could manage – when carried in its case, it reached the top of her head and hit the back of her knees. Playing a classical string instrument is the least cool thing a school pupil can do, though, and she was bullied about it, leading her to quit the lessons. She never did learn guitar and now plays no instruments.

Lipa is still remembered at Fitzjohn's and is being introduced to a new generation of pupils via the school's daily 'Wake Up, Shake Up' session. Intended to energize the youngest children by getting them singing and dancing first thing in the morning, the routine uses the 2017 single 'New Rules' as the soundtrack, albeit a version that edits out the third rule – the one about not being friends with an ex because nostalgia will see to it that you'll end up in bed with him again and having sex will set back the getting-over-him process.

When she was eleven, during the gap between finishing Year Six and starting secondary education at the highly rated Camden School for Girls, her father was offered a marketing job in Pristina. Accepting it after fourteen years in London would disrupt the family, which now included a second daughter, Rina, and a son, Gjin (born in 2001 and 2005, respectively), but doing so was part of a long-term plan. Much as Anesa and Dugi loved their adopted city, the intention had always been to return to Kosovo when they could. For Dua, it was the end of Sylvia Young and everything familiar and the start of an uncertain future in a 'foreign' country.

She was, however, a resilient kid – a trait inherited from

her parents. Unlike the average eleven-year-old facing being uprooted from the only home they've known, she was excited by the move. She and her Fitzjohn's friends were heading for different secondary schools anyway, so if she had to be taught at a place where she knew nobody, it might as well be in Kosovo. There was a bonus: in Pristina, nobody would mispronounce her name. That in itself was a big deal. To Londoners, 'Dua' was a 'weird' name, she told *NPR* in 2022, and she couldn't wait to live in a place where it wasn't.

She felt no sense of dislocation at moving from a city of 8 million to one of 205,000; nor did she mind being put in a class of older children when she arrived in Pristina. She was ahead of local eleven-year-olds due to the Kosovar practice of children starting school at six, rather than five as in the UK. On the other hand, the older pupils who were now her peers were far ahead in the sciences, and trying to compete with them was 'absolutely mortifying'. While they were tackling algebra, she was still working her way through fractions. One of the biggest obstacles, she told *NPR*, was 'learning chemistry and science and maths in a completely different language'.

It didn't matter that she already spoke Albanian; getting through a lesson in it was completely different from speaking it with her parents, and she was unable to read or write the language. Picking it up was a slow process, despite having friends who coached her, and her grades were correspondingly bad. Even after she developed a working knowledge, she misspelled words, which niggled away at the perfectionist in her. Having said that, her fluent conversational Albanian, spoken with an English accent but more than passable, ensured that there was never a period at the new school when she was unable to communicate at all.

Lipa's four years in Pristina were among the happiest of her life. She revelled in the safety and neighbourliness of Pristina, where children were allowed to walk to school alone and 'everyone knows everyone'. Her parents let her go out with friends after school without adult supervision, as long as she was back by seven o'clock. She finally got to see her father do a gig with his band; she'd been taken to many shows when he performed in London but was too young to comprehend much. When they arrived in Kosovo, he revived Oda, and she was then old enough to understand what Dad was doing on stage with a microphone and to be thrilled by the experience. Most excitingly of all, the family were watching on TV when Kosovo declared independence from Serbia in February 2008. The twelve-year-old Dua felt her parents' joy and Pristina's explosion of happiness. The celebrations could be heard across the city.

But her pride as a Kosovar kept bumping up against her ambition. Her teacher at Mileniumi i Tretë encouraged her to sing Alicia Keys and Toni Braxton songs at school, and by her early teens what had been a 'playground dream' had solidified into a plan. She knew not just that she wanted to be a musician but also that Kosovo — one of Europe's most socially isolated countries — didn't have the infrastructure to make it possible. Social media was still in its relative infancy, and she appears not even to have considered posting songs on MySpace — Lily Allen's and Adele's route to fame a couple of years earlier. 'It just didn't seem like the viral thing existed,' she told *V* magazine, looking back in 2017. What she really wanted was to be spotted and 'ship[ped] away from Kosovo', but the odds of it happening were infinitesimal.

The only way to get a career off the ground would be to return to London — and there was also the incentive of being able to resume Saturday classes at Sylvia Young. She has since said that if streaming had been a viable way of being discovered in 2010, she might have stayed in Pristina, but at the beginning of the decade, the only practical choice was to leave.

Chapter 3

SCHOOL AND BEYOND

Persuading her parents took months of delicate negotiation. Unsurprisingly: Dua was fifteen and wanted to return to London alone. Her thinking was that she'd grown up in London and had friends there, so returning would be a breeze. Her mother disagreed. Anesa Lipa had been barely out of her teens herself when she and Dukagjin moved to London, a city completely new to them, but she was implacably opposed to the idea of her daughter doing it. Once Dua had persuaded her to at least consider it, Anesa wanted to go with her, which Dua refused on the grounds that it would take her mother away from the rest of the family. (There was probably just a touch of not wanting Mum around to spoil her fun, too.)

She eventually talked them into it by framing the venture as an educational step up. Her GCSEs were coming up, and taking her exams in England, followed by A Levels a couple of years later, would improve her chances of getting into a good UK university. Presented that way, her plan seemed entirely sensible, and Dugi and Anesa could hardly refuse. To her credit, when she got to London, she did take school seriously enough to get A Levels in Politics, Psychology, Media Studies and English.

Once Lipa was famous, there was much media rehashing of this period of her life, and many headlines seized on her going to London 'alone'. The implication was that she'd not only travelled alone but lived alone when she arrived. One tabloid reported that she'd been only fourteen. She was fifteen, and she didn't live on her own – Anesa wouldn't have allowed it even if Dua had wanted to, which she didn't. Despite the audacity of her move, she was sociable and gregarious, with no interest in being completely alone.

Lipa tells two versions of the going-to-London story. In one account, she stayed with Kosovar friends of her family and was 'a really good kid', doing nothing that would worry her parents back in Pristina. They hadn't returned to London with her because her sister and brother were settled at school in Pristina, and Lipa was conscious of the degree of trust they had placed in her. The only trouble she got into in London, she said, was when she and a friend deliberately ran a towering bubble bath at the friend's flat in Marble Arch, then dropped globs of bath foam from the balcony. Foam hit a police officer who happened to be walking under the balcony, and the girls quickly learned that striking an officer of the law with bath foam counted as assault.

The telling-off they received reduced Dua to tears. She pictured herself in prison, which seemed an actual possibility. It was only when she informed the cop that she was fifteen – 'too little to go to jail' she later told an interviewer – that he relented. Instead of charging them, he said they would receive a caution, which would arrive in the post. At least she wouldn't be banged up, but a caution was bad enough. Days went by, during which she gloomily waited for the mail and pictured her mother's reaction. Anesa hadn't wanted her to go to London, and now this.

The caution never turned up, but Lipa was still gnawingly anxious that, in the interests of keeping her mother informed, the friends she was staying with would call Anesa. That didn't happen either, but it didn't mean her parents felt comfortable about her being 1,625 miles from Kosovo. Years later, she and Anesa were remembering the 'Alone in London' period and agreed that her flying the nest at fifteen had been 'scarier' than either had originally admitted. They could laugh now, but her mum, in particular, had found it very hard-going. Of course, the compensation for all the worry was that Dua became self-reliant and independent, qualities that played a huge part in getting her career off the ground, then keeping it airborne.

The second, slightly more freewheeling, version of the life-in-London story has her sharing a flat with an older Kosovar girl in Kilburn, north-west London. This friend, who was studying for her master's degree at the London School of Economics, was supposed to act as guardian but was so engrossed in her boyfriend and her studies that Dua was more or less allowed to do her own thing.

Technically, the arrangement satisfied her mother's requirement that she live with an adult, but Dua found it lacking in terms of camaraderie and just simple companionship. There were times when she would have appreciated being able to talk to her flatmate; it didn't happen, Dua says, because the other girl wasn't interested. Friction arose because of their dissimilar lifestyles. To her amazement, her flatmate once went into her room while Dua was at school and took pictures of the mess — clothes and shoes strewn around, mainly — and sent them to her mother. 'Who *does* that?' she asked *Hunger* magazine in 2015, still miffed. After that, she moved in with a friend from Sylvia Young.

The definitive details of her early months in London are hard to establish, but on arrival she did stay with family friends and then with the older girl. Turning sixteen, in August 2011, was a significant moment because in her view there was substantially more leeway: 'OK, just me and my friends now!' she said on Belgian radio in 2018. She received an allowance from her parents that offered a certain amount of freedom, but Anesa and Dugi visited London often enough to ensure that she toed the line.

What is emphasized in both accounts of the tale is how unprepared she was for the mundane reality of living without her parents. 'The cooking and cleaning was a bit of a nightmare,' she recalled; in another interview, she remembered the time her mother, visiting from Pristina, opened a wardrobe and asked what all these clothes were doing stuffed inside. They were, Dua sheepishly replied, the dirty ones she'd never got around to washing — when she ran out of clean clothes, she simply bought new ones. There was also the matter of not knowing how to use the washing machine. That went on until she eventually decided to spare her mother the pain of her closet; instead, the day before Anesa's next visit, Dua washed load after load of laundry – around six, she remembers – and thus took a step toward adulthood.

She and Anesa were exceptionally close, and her mother required daily check-ins. Dua had to phone or FaceTime when she got up in the morning, again later in the day, and if she went out at night when she returned home. 'I tried to be a good kid and tried to let them know where I was at all times,' she said. In some ways, 'kid' was the operative word; like every sixteen-year-old in the world, she assumed she was invincible, and when, inevitably, she and her friends used fake IDs to sample London nightlife, they sometimes found it dark and disconcerting. Remembering it just a few years later in her *Hunger* interview, she shrugged it off: 'I could always hold my own.'

She enrolled at Parliament Hill School in Hampstead, known to pupils as Parley, a state comprehensive for girls that also educated the *Killing Eve* actress Kirby Howell-Baptiste and comedian Grace Campbell. The latter, daughter of former Labour Party spokesman Alastair Campbell, attended at the same time as Lipa and has claimed that at school she refused to let Lipa join her gang of cool girls. The day after the 2021 Brit Awards, where Dua won the British Female Solo and British Album of the Year categories, Alastair, then a presenter on *Good Morning Britain*, laughingly compared his daughter's life and that of her former schoolmate. He told viewers that Grace had taken to doing a stand-up routine about being a former cool girl who now played pubs and clubs, while Dua is 'one of the greatest stars on the planet'. In a 2016 interview with pop culture website andPOP, Lipa diplomatically recalled the difficulty of being the new girl at school, trying to forge friendships. 'I've always been outgoing and confident but once girls create their own groups, that's it. It's that bond.'

Not being accepted by Grace Campbell's bunch seems to have left her entirely unruffled. During lunch one day at Parliament Hill, she was approached by two other girls who knew she was new. They wanted to say hello and see what she was up to, and from that moment the three were their own gang. They're still close friends to this day. The school, for its part, has never forgotten her: the day after the 2021 Grammy Awards, where she received the Pop Vocal Album prize, the *Camden New Journal* ran a story headlined 'Former Parliament Hill pupil wins Grammy Award'.

But the schoolgirl Dua knew nothing of her Grammy-filled destiny. A more immediate concern was her height. She'd been the smallest in her year at primary school and was still tiny-ish at Parliament Hill. Along with her lack of vertical stature, to her chagrin, was a figure that obstinately remained straight up and down. She watched her friends get boyfriends while she wrestled with being the one who no boy fancied, brooding that she might never grow. Unexpectedly, when she was eighteen, she added an extra six or so inches, ending up 5ft 8in (revealing her height during an interview, she added that her shoe size was six. Luckily for her, she avoided the usual tall-girl trial of hard-to-fit big feet).

She was enthusiastic at school, and even more so in her free time. At seventeen, having observed the development of fashion blogging, she launched her own site, Dua Daily. It existed both as an outlet for her thoughts about clothes and style – a fashion fan since childhood, she had many thoughts – and as a means of getting noticed by the music business. She hadn't given up her dream of becoming a singer; Dua Daily was a way of getting the word out, first by drawing attention to songs she was posting on YouTube (more on this later) and then by keeping readers updated as her career slowly began to move.

The original Daily, hosted on the Blogspot platform, is gone now, but a fragment survives on the Lookbook website. The 'about me' section says, sweetly, 'London based fashion daily blogger, aspiring singer.' A couple of photos, dated 2012, show her out and about at night, with everything she's wearing carefully annotated ('Disco pants, navy blue, American Apparel').

She tended it regularly for several years, even as her career began to gather pace, and her blog entries reflected her life as it changed. The earlier Dailys were a schoolgirl's diary of what she was up to and what clothes she'd bought that week; later, the tone changed, and it was no longer about shopping trips. Now, she was musing about the importance of networking. Even if 'networking' was what used to be called just 'going out and meeting people', she wasn't wrong. The ability to talk to important people was one of her innate skills, and she instantly perceived that it would be the key to success, either as a blogger or a musician. Dua Daily didn't turn her into a big-name fashion blogger like Rookie's Tavi Gevinson or David 'High Snobiety' Fischer, but it offered plenty of networking practice as she interacted with followers and influencers.

Thanks to having spent much of her study time socializing and blogging, Dua's A Level results were disappointing. After enrolling in an intensive one-year revision course, she retook the exams. According to the *Wall Street Journal*, she got top marks the second time and set about applying to universities. Four accepted her, putting her in a tricky situation. She'd resat her A Levels and filled in the admission forms to prove to herself that she could meet the challenge; having met it, she now wanted to defer her place for a year and concentrate on putting demos and cover versions online in the hope of finding a manager.

She'd been sporadically posting on Twitter and SoundCloud for several years, and she had her own YouTube channel, but now she planned to redouble her efforts, as long as her parents went along with the idea of a gap year. She presented the deferment as a win-win proposition: she would either get her foot in the door of the music business or she would go to university. Anesa and Dukagjin agreed on the understanding that if her gap year didn't pan out, she really *would* go to university, no quibbling. The year passed, and it was put up or shut up time. While she'd made progress with the music, she wasn't where she wanted to be, and according to the agreement with her parents, this was when she'd have to quit music or at least relegate it to side-project status. Yet she had no desire to study something she wasn't passionate about, and she had to break the news to Dukagjin and Anesa that the gap year was going to be a gap life.

Their response was exactly what she'd expected. 'My parents were like, "Are you kidding me?"' she related to *Harper's Bazaar*. The elder Lipas greatly valued education, especially when the alternative would be struggle and uncertainty. Dugi had a unique perspective on it: he'd had that Yugoslavian hit single when he was sixteen but never reached the point where he could make a living from music alone. Dua had generational advantages that he hadn't, like social media and streaming platforms, but he and Anesa were dubious about her chances. They suggested she tried working on her music at the same time as going to university, but Dua was adamant. There was no Plan B; if there was something to fall back on, she'd fail to focus on her goal.

That has been her career philosophy all along: 'No Plan B.' It's Plan A or nothing, and if Plan A doesn't work out, it just wasn't meant to be. She was so set on becoming a musician, and so certain she could pull it off, that she never even considered another career. Not for her the security of a fallback job; there would be no training for another profession. Her musician father had reluctantly studied dentistry in Pristina just to have an alternative occupation, but Dua wouldn't, or couldn't. Asked by *Miss Vogue* what her own alternative occupation would be, she laughed: 'A fairy princess.'

'No Plan B' had actually been her father's motto; it was he who'd pointed out to her the wisdom of concentrating on her aims without the distraction of a backup. He was speaking from his own disappointing experience — he *had* fallen back on Plan B, but giving up his own dream had made him hope his daughter wouldn't have to do the same.

She and her parents were extraordinarily close, then and now. Anesa was twenty-three and Dukagjin twenty-six when Dua was born, but their youthfulness was tempered by maturity – a consequence of having lived as refugees but also, it appears, because that's simply who they were. They may have been young parents, listening to rock and funk around the house and encouraging their daughter's creativity, but they also expected her to be mannerly and productive. Dua adored them. Her mother, she has said, 'is an angel from heaven', and the bond is emphasized by an 'ANGEL' tattoo on Dua's right arm.

Her father, meanwhile, is her 'twin' – the word she used in her Instagram birthday greeting to him in March 2022, when he turned fifty-three – and not just because of their physical resemblance. When Dua unexpectedly severed ties with longtime managers Ben Mawson and Ed Millett in February 2022, at the start of the Future Nostalgia tour, she's said to have asked Dugi to take over her management (this was reported by the UK media but has not been officially confirmed). If he *is* managing Dua, he certainly isn't the first parent to oversee a famous offspring's career. His professional qualifications are in marketing and communications, which are transferable skills; he also has his personal music-industry experience with Oda, and, of course, he spent years occupying a front-row seat as his daughter rose to superstardom. All told, those aren't bad credentials.

He and Anesa are tireless workers, sharing values and pushed by a need to help their beloved Kosovo. It was rare that Dua fell out with either of them; most disagreements were settled by compromising. (She wanted to pierce her belly button; fine, said her mother, as long as you get an A in maths.) But the university vs career wrangle was, as Dua saw it, unavoidable.

Financially speaking, Dua was already semi-independent by then. She has said that, at sixteen, she worked in Mayfair, London, as a nightclub greeter – the person with the clipboard and ear-piece who tells you you're not on the list. It takes 'a cold person', as she put it, to do it; the club's management were in her ear, telling her to let that one in but keep that one out, and often the ones who were rejected were fine apart from some minor transgression like wearing trainers. That was the exact reason she was forced to turn away a group of her friends one night, and it was then that she acknowledged that she wasn't cold enough for the job. The next one was a waitressing gig at La Bodega Negra, a Mexican street-food restaurant in Soho. 'I walked Channing Tatum and his wife to a table once. Good times!' she laughed when asked about it by the BBC in 2016. Crushingly for Tatum, she added that he was better looking on-screen than in the flesh.

And during her free time, starting when she was fifteen, she was recording demos in a friend's boyfriend's bedroom studio. Nearly all were cover versions, though she'd also been writing her own material since the age of fourteen. Only one self-written song survives online: a 1.5-minute snippet called 'Lions & Tigers & Bears' – her tribute to one of her favourite films, *The Wizard of Oz*. It's been on SoundCloud since 2012, and Lipa keeps it there as a kind of historical document – her first piece of original songwriting. For a fourteen-year-old, she was adept at writing dramatic melody lines, but her startlingly mature voice is the selling point. The tenderness as she ascends the melody, and the tremor as she hits the top, bespeak years of singing to herself at home.

Lipa went back to it a year or so later, teaming up with Ryan Laubscher, a producer who had done sessions with Pixie Lott and Geri Halliwell. She contacted him — years later, he still had the email she'd sent — and the two made some progress in the studio. A longer version of the track can be heard on Laubscher's YouTube channel, but it didn't come to much. 'In the end,' Lipa told *Spin* magazine, 'he decided that he didn't need a pop act to develop, and he didn't want to work with me.'

For unknown singers like her, cover versions were a better discovery mechanism than original songs, anyway. She filled her YouTube channel with them. In fact, their purpose was twofold. She wanted to be noticed by the music industry, but equally importantly, she wanted to show her mates that she could sing. Drawing her friends' attention to her YouTube work was a statement: here's a song I've covered and uploaded; now you know that I really can sing and I'm not just messing around. And if you want to spread the word about my videos, that would be much appreciated.

The hope was that, somehow, it would lead to bigger things. But she was realistic. As passionate and determined as she was, she knew she had an uphill battle ahead. 'I thought [pop success] was as far-fetched as cartoon characters on TV,' she told *NME*'s Nick Levine in 2017.

Nevertheless, she kept posting on YouTube on the off chance that someone in the industry would spot her. But it 'never had that Justin Bieber effect I was hoping for', she told America's ABC News in 2018. Bieber had pioneered the phenomenon of being discovered by putting videos online – after a year on YouTube, in 2008 he came to the attention of manager Scooter Braun, and by the time he turned sixteen he was world-famous. All that any young hopeful needed to get herself onto YouTube was basic editing skills, and Lipa, with her haunting voice, thought she was in with a shot. But thousands of others had the same idea, and she hadn't yet acquired the singularity that would have made her videos stand out.

What she *did* have, though, as revealed by a clip filmed early in 2017, was an understanding of her voice and how she wanted to sound. The video shows her covering Etta James's 1967 blues classic 'I'd Rather Go Blind', and it is notable that she stops several times to confer with the producer, because she knows she's capable of better. She was already signed to Warner Bros. Records by then, and the song would appear on an EP called *Live Acoustic* in December 2017, but the online footage offers a rare glimpse of her early recording process. *Live Acoustic* also contains a version of Amy Winehouse's 'Tears Dry On Their Own' that's barely distinguishable from the original, so closely does Lipa follow Winehouse's phrasing. Between the two songs, 'Blind' and 'Tears', Lipa finds a soulful depth that isn't present in her dance songs. We hear her voice's underlying strength and the subtlety that balances it.

The covers she uploaded as an ambitious fifteen-year-old were a mixed bag picked to show her range. They included

Christina Aguilera's bluesy throwback 'Ain't No Other Man', the Joss Stone soul belter 'Super Duper Love', Jessie J's poppy 'Price Tag' and the dance floor-ready 'Say My Name' by Destiny's Child — each a big, bravura number that demanded to be sung with conviction. Her 'Say My Name' video typified her Gen Z style: she filmed herself sitting cross-legged on her bed, wearing a hoodie and reading the lyrics from her laptop, which was in front of her on the bed. Even bent over the laptop — the least effective way to deliver a song in terms of breath control — she's powerful and focused, but also immersed in the task as if there were no greater fun to be had anywhere. Though talented and attractive, she's also relatable, the kind of girl who inspires others her age to have a go themselves.

And that's exactly what happened. Once she became a name in her own right, fans posted videos of themselves singing her songs for the same reason she'd done it herself: to make someone notice. Touched, she listened to as many as she could, noting that the next big pop star might be out there, covering her tunes.

Even at fifteen, she had a visual trademark: each song was introduced with 'I'm Dua, I'm fifteen' — and then 'Mwah!' 'Mwah!' was intended as an insouciant kissy greeting to those watching the video, and she clearly liked the word: it also found its way into the 2016 single 'Blow Your Mind (Mwah)'. On the latter, though, it was employed as a lethargic kiss-off to a boyfriend who didn't appreciate her — there's an utter lack of energy in her 'mwah', as if she can't be bothered to muster a sarcastic or angry one. In the accompanying video, she wore a MWAH choker, the word spelled out in three-inch-high crystal letters. For a while, it was available to buy in her online merchandise store – the perfect statement piece.

(The MWAH choker is no longer in stock, but the shop does offer a delicate gold Sugaboo necklace for £20/$25, including velvet bag with an embroidered Dua Lipa logo. The word 'sugaboo' was a made-up endearment interchangeably used by Lipa and two of her co-writers, Sarah Hudson and Clarence Coffee, while working on the song 'Levitating' in 2018. It found its way into the 'Levitating' lyric, and as a tribute Coffee and Hudson had a Sugaboo necklace made for Lipa's twenty-fifth birthday in 2020. It sparked enough interest that she made it available through her store.)

Lipa was shown rewatching those early YouTube videos in a 2016 documentary called *See in Blue* (produced by the American magazine *The Fader*). She appeared mildly embarrassed by her fifteen-year-old earnestness. She regarded the mix of musical styles – Jessie J, Destiny's Child, et al. – as a sign that she hadn't yet found her own sound, and she wasn't keen on her schoolgirlish presentation style – the 'I'm Dua, mwah' part of it. It's normal to be mortified by seeing evidence of your teenage behaviour, but the point of uploading cover versions onto YouTube is that young hopefuls are showing their talent at its rawest before professional writers and producers get hold of it.

She continued to show her YouTube material to friends, to little avail. Eventually, she abandoned the idea that her home-made videos could be the entrée she was seeking and instead kept them as 'a form of portfolio', sending them to producers and writers whose work she admired with a request that they contact her if they liked the music. She became increasingly proactive in that direction, going to gigs at, say, KOKO in Camden — her local venue — and striking up conversations with likely looking people. If they turned out to be a producer or songwriter, she directed them to her portfolio, and so began to make connections. One of the great moments of her career, she said much later, was headlining KOKO in her own right, in October 2016. Her world had shifted on its axis; she was no longer the girl behind the barrier in the audience, watching the likes of J. Cole or Bruno Mars on stage and screaming the lyrics. Standing on that stage herself was 'life-changing', she said. Its capacity of 1,410 was one-fifteenth the size of venues she would eventually play, but it was her local, the one whose website she had checked every week, and playing there was a Damascene moment she's never forgotten.

If her 'portfolio' phase taught her anything, it was the value of slogging. Approaching people at gigs on the off chance that they might be in the industry took guts, and she did it over and over. In Jarvis Cocker's 2022 autobiography *Good Pop, Bad Pop*, the Pulp singer recalled attending gigs with a cassette tape in his pocket, ready to thrust it at anyone who might be interested in an untested young group from Sheffield. One night he managed to hand one to Radio 1 presenter John Peel, venerated gatekeeper to the station's indie coverage. Pulp were invited to record a session for Peel's show, starting their lengthy, ultimately triumphant climb to the top of British pop. Lipa's portfolio was the twenty-first-century version of Cocker's cassette. 'I think it was really just to show persistence and that I was really invested in this,' she told *Paper* magazine in 2017.

Lipa invested impressive energy into shopping around the portfolio and it contributed to her success by providing a grounding in how to meet people, but the real breakthrough was unrelated to her efforts in that direction. It happened during the brief time she was signed to a modelling agency, which sent her on go-sees for potential jobs. One day the go-see was a casting for an X *Factor* TV ad. She couldn't have known it then, but it would make all the difference.

Chapter 4

GETTING SIGNED

London is teeming with attractive young women, and Lipa was one of them. But she also had a freshness and vivacity that made it almost certain that she'd be scouted by a model agent. It happened at Topshop in Oxford Circus, then the prime weekend hangout for fashion-conscious girls, and modelling didn't seem like a bad idea at that point. A few of her friends were doing it, and it was also a way – she hoped – to make connections in the music business while earning cash to sustain her until she broke through. That, anyway, was the plan. She didn't meet anyone who could help her with her music, but she did get a few jobs, including the ASOS Marketplace online catalogue and a TV ad for the 2013 series of the *X Factor*.

To herald the tenth series of the reality singing competition, broadcast that autumn and won by Sam Bailey, ITV commissioned a promo that would 'highlight the talent'. The ad agency tasked with making the commercial, which was titled 'Our Star', were asked to find 'a new star, one that would be loved by the nation'. What that boiled down to was casting an actress/singer who looked as if she could be one of the thousands of girls who try out for the show every year – but with greater charisma. Lipa's agency thought she might fit the brief: she sang, had the requisite girl-next-door look and was strikingly personable. She went to the casting in Soho and got a callback the same day. A few days later, she went to producer Jake Gosling's Sticky Studios in Windlesham, Surrey, to record her vocals for the song being used in the advert, Sister Sledge's 'Lost in Music'. The 1979 tune was co-written by Nile Rodgers, and in the intersectional way of the music business, in 2019 Lipa would write a song with him that, unfortunately, hasn't yet been released.

A behind-the-scenes clip made by the ad agency captured her excitement. She was filmed in Gosling's studio, arguably the most ebullient person in the room, explaining that she'd gone to a casting, got the callback and, well, here she was. Her nervous giggle was understandable: after three years of singing in bedroom studios, it was sensational to be making a professional recording.

That, however, was nothing compared to the thrill of filming the ad, which took place in an ordinary London back garden. 'We are on set,' she says in an I-can't-believe-any-of-this tone, standing in the garden as workers set up shots and marshal extras. 'It's such a massive crew. Such a massive crew.' 'Massive' was right.

Dozens were involved: camera ops, lighting people, sound techs, producers, directors, assistants, caterers, a crane operator for aerial shots – and that's not counting somewhere around 100 extras.

She plays an average teenager, daydreaming about pop stardom while hanging out the washing. Sorting through the laundry basket, she begins to sing 'Lost in Music' and gets fully drawn into the song, treating it like a stage performance. Hitting the high notes with vigour and reaching a passionate crescendo, she's unaware that the entire street can hear her and that it's causing a commotion.

She's styled to look like an everygirl: hair casually twisted into a bun, pink earbuds connected to a 2013 iPod (probably – we don't see the actual device hidden under her oversized T-shirt). Her singing draws a larger and larger crowd until half the neighbourhood is standing outside the garden, wondering who's warbling. Two schoolgirls on a bus watch her performance on a phone and sing along; at a nearby block of high-rise flats, a girl unfurls a banner saying 'WE HEART OUR STAR', and in a convenience store someone puts up a poster with Dua's face surrounded by the words, 'She's got the X Factor'. A TV in a living room is tuned to the X Factor's sister programme, the Xtra Factor, and presenter Caroline Flack is exclaiming, 'Here on the Xtra Factor, we love her!'

In the ad, Dua makes it as far as an audition in front of the judges (that year: Gary Barlow, Nicole Scherzinger, Louis Walsh and Sharon Osbourne), and the message, brilliantly embodied by the then seventeen-year-old singer, is that anyone could be 'our star'. Anyone, that is, apart from an artist like Dua, who was committed to making her name in her own way rather than via the talent-show route. She wasn't snobbish about acts who did get a leg up from the *X Factor* or *Britain's Got Talent*. Rather, she was realistic — if there were no other way for a singer to be heard, then why not? It's an opportunity, like any other.

Around that time, Lipa was frequently 'offered' — by whom she doesn't say — the chance to compete on talent shows herself. She was told it would be an efficient way to be seen and to find a manager — a genuine incentive, because getting representation was near the top of her agenda. But she was too engrossed in making her own music, which wouldn't have meshed with the *X Factor* cover-versions policy, and she also felt pretty sure that she could land a manager if she kept trying under her own steam.

Nevertheless, being in the commercial was 'an absolute blast', she says. Its director, Oscar Cariss, lavishes praise on her, saying she was 'incredible, for a seventeen-year-old. She has incredible confidence; she's just been a joy to work with.' The behind-the-scenes clip finishes with Lipa remarking that the *X Factor* had launched when she was seven (in fact, it started in 2004, when she was nine), and now here she was, in the commercial.

The ad itself didn't turn Lipa into a household name, and she didn't do another because she left the modelling agency soon afterward. She says it was because the agency instructed her to lose 'a lot of weight', and she was disinclined to do so, seeing modelling merely as a means to an end rather than a career.

But if the ad didn't make her famous, it set in motion the

events that did. The eminently well-connected Jake Gosling, whose production CV includes Ed Sheeran, Lady Gaga and One Direction, was impressed by her voice and wondered if she'd be interested in a publishing deal. This being totally new territory for her, she called a lawyer to discuss it and decided not to take the deal. There's an unverifiable story that she was also offered a contract by Simon Cowell and his Syco label, which she is also said to have declined; what is definitely true is that Cowell later got plenty of ribbing for having Lipa right there under his nose and 'letting her get away', as Radio 1 DJ Greg James put it. The lawyer informed her that, before anything else, she needed a manager. She actually googled 'managers' before the lawyer introduced her to Ben Mawson, whose company TaP Management had represented Lana Del Rey since 2009. Once Lipa began to make a name for herself, the media searched for similarities with Del Rey— a fruitless task, because as artists they couldn't be more dissimilar.

By the time she met Mawson and his business partner Ed Millett, she was already having discussions with other companies. It was 2013, a few months after the X Factor ad. She was now eighteen, and it was increasingly evident that there was something special about this enterprising girl from north-west London who was astute enough to see her old videos as not just a cluster of disparate tracks but a collection of work. Moreover, if she could turn 'Lost in Music' into her own artistic moment, imagine what she'd be able to do with a tune in which she felt truly invested.

Her potential was immense—and she knew it. When Mawson asked what she wanted to achieve, she said, 'I want to be as big as

Madonna.' Mawson, an ambitious type himself, liked her attitude and competitiveness, and he and Millett got her signature. It was one of their best management calls: these days, Lipa isn't quite as big as Madonna — nobody is — but she's big enough to request Madonna's participation on a collaboration (a remix of 'Levitating' which also features Missy Elliott) and for Madonna to say yes.

Mawson put her to work immediately. 'Literally the day after [she signed with TaP],' Lipa told *Rolling Stone*, they organized writing sessions for her — Lipa's first experience of writing in a professional environment. They also signed her to a publishing contract, Lipa being the first artist that TaP both managed and published, and as of early 2023 her name is still on their publishing roster. The most notable song that came out of the early sessions was 'Hotter than Hell', which is still in her personal Top 10 of her favourite songs. It would be released as the fourth single from her debut album, *Dua Lipa*, and reach No. 15 in the UK chart.

Though not her biggest sales hit, the song was a stepping stone, regarded by Lipa as one of the most important of this incubatory stint of her career. Until 'Hotter than Hell', she'd been casting around for a musical identity, a problem that had increasingly consumed her while posting covers on YouTube. She'd had an idea that she wanted to sound like a cross between rapper J. Cole and her early-teens hero Nelly Furtado, a fusion that raised eyebrows when she mentioned it to producers. Other attempts to describe what she wanted were muddled — all she knew was that she liked pop melodies and hip-hop's flow, but she couldn't pinpoint a way of bringing them together.

Without a style to call her own, she was just another pop singer, albeit one with a voice deeper and richer than most. Then 'Hotter than Hell' came along. Co-written with Adam Midgley, Tommy Baxter and Gerard O'Connell (who also release music in their own right as Ritual), it was sultry and faintly menacing. Like a number of Dua songs, it was inspired by a former boyfriend who'd made her feel that her best wasn't good enough. The label she would eventually adopt to describe her sound was 'dark pop', and 'Hotter than Hell' qualified – the term had come to her as she worked on it.

Previously, she had toyed with calling her sound 'progressive pop', which brings to mind early seventies synthesizer bands. This 'dark pop' wasn't a new coinage; the label had been used for decades to describe synth-based songs written in a minor key, the definitive example of pre-Lipa dark pop being the *Twin Peaks* theme tune 'Falling', recorded by Julee Cruise. This definition didn't apply to 'Hotter than Hell' in any sense, but Lipa's concept changed the term's meaning. To her, dark pop combined upful melodies and introspective lyrics, and she later said that the artist who best personifies it is Sia. At that moment in the studio, though, midway through creating 'Hotter than Hell', she finally had her own genre, and it was a milestone.

The song was hard to nail down, however. In the throes of heartache after a break-up, she was determined to come up with a sad song. The idea of a gut-spilling weepie appealed more than anything else, until she actually sat down to write it. Though vulnerability can produce the strongest songs, she had a lightbulb moment. Rather than focusing on weakness, how about if she rejigged it so the unworthy boyfriend returned to her because he just couldn't get her out of his head? How about, say, letting him pine for her while she coolly toyed with him – sometimes she was there for him, devilishly hot and lustful, but at other times she absented herself and enjoyed the idea of him 'burning' for her?

Once she stopped seeing herself as the victim and began imagining the schmuck of an ex as a pitiable figure, she felt a surge of power. But she found that the chorus wasn't coming together and after struggling with it for days was on the verge of abandoning the whole thing. Then, scrolling through Tumblr one day, she saw the words 'Hotter than Hell' – red letters, black background. With that, she had the missing piece: she wasn't just desirable, she was hotter than hell.

Those three words became both the chorus and the title of the song. Up till the Tumblr moment, the phrase 'hotter than hell' hadn't even occurred to her, but it perfectly encapsulated her state of mind, and the alliteration was punchy. She and her co-writers were able to finish the song, and as soon as they had she felt a hum of energy about it that distinguished it from others she'd written. It was the first that felt like a true reflection of herself: sensitive but powerful, conflicted but, in the long run, sure of herself. It would help to shape her debut album.

When people were finally able to hear it, a couple of years later – it was released for downloading and streaming in May 2016, reaching No. 15 in the UK singles chart – many found it empowering. One encounter stuck with her for a long time: a fan approached her in Stockholm and said the song had changed her life. Dua was flattered and surprised. Writing 'Hotter than Hell' had been a step forward in her emotional development – the word she used was 'therapeutic' – but it hadn't occurred to her that anything so personal might have relevance to others. At that moment, she had an inkling of her power, accompanied by the realization that everyone (pop stars, fans, everyone) goes through the same experiences. 'Maybe if I'm honest and tell my stories, maybe the fans will see that we all feel the same thing, in the hopes that you can relate to it,' she said in 2018, during a Q&A session hosted by Miami radio station Hits 97.3.

In the meantime, she pressed on with the writing sessions arranged by Ben Mawson and quickly came up against a logistical problem. She was working nights at La Bodega Negra, getting home late, then having to wake up early to go to the sessions. Not that she was complaining. If anything, she was having a whale of a time. From her point of view it was an ideal existence, because after work she was partying with friends and – thanks to the limitless energy of a nineteen-year-old – only needed a few hours' sleep before hitting the studio the next day. Yet after ploughing on for a while, it became obvious that she'd have to leave her job. When she quit, she was diplomatic about it, not wanting to burn her bridges in case she ever needed to go back. As she put it, who knew what was going to happen with her music career?

To tide her over, TaP paid her a monthly salary. She didn't need much to live on, Mawson noted, and the salary kept her focused on writing. Lipa herself was overjoyed in a living-the-dream way; being able to spend her days working on music was almost unbelievable. Even so, money was tight, and for part of each month she lived on supermarket meal deals – the sandwich/snack/drink combo offered by most chains for around £5. Chelcee Grimes, a co-writing partner since 2014 – among their collaborations are 'Love Again' and 'Kiss and Make Up' – reminisced to the *Mirror* in 2020 about the pair's experience of 'being skint in London'. It wasn't pleasant, Grimes said, but adversity can be a great driver of creativity, and she and Lipa bonded during their dinner-from-Tesco experience.

The story provoked eyerolls from some *Mirror* readers, one of whom tweeted, 'Tesco meal deals – what a bloody luxury! I survived on bread and dripping!' Asked for a budget-meal tip after the *Mirror* story came out, Lipa recommended beans on toast – still one of her favourites even now.

In mid-2014, with 'Hotter than Hell' recorded, her managers began to let the industry know they were developing a special new talent. They weren't ready to let labels hear her, but Warner Music was interested, sight unseen. Lacking a major female pop star, the company wanted to find one to compete in a very strong era of talent that included Rihanna, Katy Perry, Lady Gaga and Ariana Grande. Joe Kentish, who had just become head of A&R (artists and repertoire), had a general catch-up meeting at Mawson's office to find out what he was currently up to. Specifically, Kentish wanted to know about this pop-star-in-waiting he'd heard about, but he was told that it was still early days and he wouldn't be able to hear the music till further down the line. Here, fate intervened.

While Kentish was in Mawson's office, Lipa unexpectedly dropped by to sign papers. If she hadn't, he probably wouldn't have heard the songs, let alone met her, for weeks.

She was, he told the Burstimo Marketing *Music Industry* podcast in December 2020, 'a bundle of energy'. Once they'd been introduced, she asked whether he'd heard a hip-hop song she liked and spontaneously rapped the whole track for him, winning him over by sheer force of personality. 'I just thought, "This is exciting."' Lipa's rap flow can be heard on a cover of Chance the Rapper's 'Cocoa Butter Kisses', posted on her SoundCloud in 2013 and still online. She apologetically explained that she limited her vocal to 'a one-tone range' because rapping was 'adventurous enough' without bringing voice-gymnastics into it. Her take on the song is leisurely and sensual, arguably more so than Chance's original.

Lipa was exactly the kind of proposition Kentish could work with. His speciality was helping to develop artists who already had a strong sense of who they were; he knew the producers and writers who would bring out the best in them and what each party could bring to the table. Lipa's talent, Kentish's skill as a nurturer and a connection to the right people, plus Warner Music's industry heft, made them an ideal fit.

The label offered a deal on the spot, which rarely happens. But it made sense for Warner's and for Lipa: she had a cluster of songs ready to go and a clear idea of what she wanted to do, so Warner's would be getting an artist who was already some way down the development path. In return, they would treat her as a priority from the moment she signed the contract.

They were so keen to find a mainstream female pop artist that Kentish had been specifically tasked with the job. The company had been a force in pop in the past, with Madonna having once been on the roster, and it was set on being one again. What they wanted, in the words of company chairman Miles Leonard, was 'another Madonna', and in Lipa they found their star.

In effect, though, the label took a punt. Despite having several strong songs by then, and an overwhelmingly can-do attitude, she didn't have an undeniable smash hit – like, say, 'New Rules', which wouldn't be recorded until 2017 – among her demos. Still, the label judged the songs she did have, headed by 'Hotter than Hell', strong enough, and Lipa was charismatic and highly likeable.

Getting her wasn't a completely streamlined process, with other labels also pitching after Warner Bros. Records submitted its offer. Dugi Lipa, who closely observed the process, said two more majors made serious offers, but Warner's closed the deal because their package was most attractive. They were able to promise her a lane of her own – there were no other female pop singers on the roster to siphon away resources, so she would have Kentish's undivided attention. That amounted to a precious advantage in the life of a rising pop star; many new acts, and even some established ones, find themselves lost in the shuffle at times, with overworked A&R people spreading themselves too thinly. Dua would know that Kentish was always there for her.

Once she signed the deal – an occasion so momentous that she flew her parents to London from Kosovo so they could watch – a pile of work awaited her and the label. One of the hardest jobs in A&R is pairing pop singers with the right material, and because she wanted to write her own songs, her writing needed polishing. She was already pretty good (see 'Hotter than Hell'), and in Ben Mawson's experience that made her better than plenty of more seasoned writers. Some manage 'half a good song' in ten sessions, he told *Music Business Worldwide* in 2018, whereas Lipa comes up with something complete and excellent every fourth or fifth time.

Nevertheless, Kentish's vision, shared by Lipa and Mawson, was that she would be known not simply for great pop bops but for songs that were interesting and different. It was a tall order at a time when much pop music relied on the same tropes and melodic structures. She already had the ideas, but what she lacked was the studio experience necessary to develop as a writer, and she faced a dauntingly steep learning curve. Kentish estimated that the average professional pop songwriter has at least 10,000 hours of studio writing time under their belt, and Lipa, for all her industriousness, had a long way to go. It took close to a year to build up a respectable number of hours, and there was a period when there wasn't much tangible improvement. She carried on, five days a week, doggedly putting in the time. Quitting wasn't in her nature, and she refused to countenance the idea that she might not be up to it. She pressed on by increments, looking for the sound that was different and unique to her—in effect, melding 'dark pop' into what Kentish called 'her narrative'.

One of the most challenging things was arriving at a session where she knew no one and being expected to instantly feel a rapport. It could be 'really scary', she said, building a sense of intimacy out of nothing in order to create. Writing often started with a simple conversation about how she was feeling and what she'd been doing, and from there a topic might be teased out and a song might develop. It was imperative that she be honest during these initial chats, because if she weren't, the resulting song would be based on a false version of herself and that was, for her, unthinkable. She strongly believed — it was almost the pillar around which everything else flowed at the sessions — that her material had to be truthful.

That had much to do with her love of hip-hop, a genre based on the tenet 'be real'. Its truthfulness was a great influence on her. Even at nineteen, funnelled into rooms with writers who had done this for years, she felt there was no alternative to pouring out her feelings. That code of honesty was the reason she still loved Nelly Furtado and P!nk: their music had never stopped being candid, even when candour provoked difficult conversations in real life. P!nk's 2002 single 'Family Portrait', to take one example, depicted her parents' marriage so pitilessly that her mother and father, by then divorced, cried when she played it to them.

Nevertheless, Dua walked into many sessions and found that she and the other writers 'didn't really vibe', she told Popjustice. The main problem was the one-sidedness — the expectation that she would confide in people she'd only just met, with no reciprocation. She quickly developed a routine to make things more productive, or at least less awkward. Though the songs were supposed to reflect her experiences, she began to ask the others about their own lives, turning the session into a conversation in which all parties were equal. Getting to know them made it easier to open up about herself.

Once comfortable, Lipa had plenty to talk about. Her romantic relationships were an obvious subject: around that time, she was dating a London-based chef/model, Isaac Carew. Lipa has never revealed what songs he might have inspired, and it's been the same for each subsequent relationship. There haven't been many, and, unusually for a pop celebrity, Lipa rarely discusses who she's seeing, even when asked directly by interviewers. Thus, there's little mileage in gossipy stories about this boyfriend or that one. The best the media have been able to come up with was a report in 2018 that a then boyfriend was seen kissing another girl in a club while Lipa's song 'One Kiss' played over the PA (a juicy scenario, but Lipa has never commented).

After Carew, she spent six months with Paul Klein of the American indie band LANY, then two years with Anwar Hadid, model brother of Bella and Gigi. Since splitting with Hadid at the end of 2021, she's been single, though in late 2022 there were reports that she was dating American rapper Jack Harlow. Nearly a year after she and Hadid uncoupled she remarked that it was the longest interval she'd had between relationships. It was great to be able to concentrate solely on herself, which she'd never had the chance to do before. She made the comments on her podcast, *Dua Lipa: At Your Service* (launched in February 2022, along with the Service95 newsletter), and they felt like a retort to media suggestions that she was seeing Trevor Noah, a South African comic and until the end of 2022 host of the American satirical news programme *The Daily Show*. He'd been a guest on *At Your Service* in October 2022, discussing his memoir *Born a Crime*, and the two were photographed hugging on a New York street corner. Other than that, there wasn't much evidence that they were dating.

None of her relationships has been a headline-grabber – there have been no wineglass-flinging break-ups or public arguments – and the only bit of near-gossip she's ever provided was when she called one of her exes 'boring'. It was two days after the 2018 Brit Awards, where she'd won in the British Breakthrough Act and British Female Solo Artist categories, and she confided to an interviewer that, unlike another former boyfriend, this 'boring' one hadn't sent a congratulatory text. But it was fine, because she didn't want to hear from him anyway.

With no real romantic drama to report, the media must make do with the occasional shot of Lipa and her partner of the moment arm-in-arm at some event. She's so circumspect that, before posting shots of her and Hadid on Instagram, she would ask if he minded.

While writing for her first album, she also drew inspiration from friends' lives, and from the Bodega Negra job she'd just left. That in itself provided much to chew over. She witnessed 'dramas every night, the dark side of nightlife', she told the *Guardian*. 'It's a good time to be making music that is seductive and sweet but doesn't sugar-coat it.'

Perhaps inevitably, her openness couldn't last. Looking forward a few years after the debut, a very different writing process is revealed. As her fame grew, she found it necessary to be more veiled about her personal life when writing, and by the time she began work on *Future Nostalgia* in early 2018, the chief priority had become keeping certain things private. The relationship with Hadid, whom she started seeing in mid-2019, was completely off-limits as song fodder. Or rather, there were no direct references to it.

To clarify: where debut album *Dua Lipa* was practically a diary of real-life feelings and events, *Future Nostalgia* was based on universal emotions of love and desire unrelated to events in her own life. If they *had* been inspired by her life, it was impossible to tell, because there was nothing in the lyrics that could be read as 'personal'. The change was noticed by Sarah Hudson, co-writer of the *FN* single 'Levitating', who told the *Los Angeles Times* that while Lipa's performance lavished the song with 'real star quality', she was also 'slightly mysterious' about deeply held thoughts.

Back in 2014, there was another early breakthrough when she jettisoned the idea that she should be writing tunes specifically for radio. Having come up with 'Hotter than Hell', the song responsible for getting her signed and a 'radio song' by any definition, Lipa felt that everything she wrote should have the same instantly catchy, hit-in-waiting quality. When Lipa makes a decision, she throws everything into it, and for a while she arrived at each session with the specific aim of Writing a Hit. The stress made it impossible to let loose and create. It was only when she abandoned the idea and concentrated on what came naturally that she began to enjoy songwriting, and the tunes duly flowed.

Ironically, once she became fully immersed in the *Dua Lipa* sessions, she ran up against a problem she couldn't have anticipated: now that she was spending so much time in the studio, she didn't have anything to write about. She felt 'jaded' – real life outside the sessions had in effect been put on hold, and that was a problem for a writer who relied so heavily on give-and-take between herself and her friends. On the upside, her skills had come on markedly, so she was sent to North America to work with a fresh group of professionals. In 2015 alone, she went to Los Angeles four times and New York nearly as often. It was in the latter city that she created 'New Love' with writers/producers Emile Haynie and Andrew Wyatt, both veterans and both sympathetic to what she wanted to convey. That was easy: after a year of dogged effort, what she wanted to show was her worry that the music business had no place for her and that it would all be for nothing. 'New Love' was released online on the day before her twentieth birthday, in August 2015, and while it didn't do much sales-wise, it did bring her to the attention of tastemakers. Their support led to her nomination for the BBC Sound of 2016 award.

When she finally cracked the writing code and was comfortable with producing lyrics that were genuinely close to her heart, the rest of the sessions came fairly easily. On a trip to Toronto in October 2014, she was introduced to producer/writer Stephen 'Koz' Kozmeniuk, whose credits then included Madonna, Nicki Minaj and Meek Mill (he would also produce 'Space Man', the 2022 song performed by Sam Ryder that gave Britain its best Eurovision result since 1998). She had already spent the day writing with another team, but Koz was young and came highly recommended, so she reluctantly agreed to work with him that evening.

She was too tired to enjoy the session, and at first she wasn't keen on the song that came out of it, either. It was 'Last Dance', which would eventually be released as her third single, but right then and there Lipa knew only that she was knackered and fed up and didn't much care about this tune she, Koz and British songwriter Talay Riley had just come up with. Go forward a few months, after she'd recorded it and listened back to the fully produced item, and she had completely changed her mind. In her exhaustion and vulnerability, she had created the song that became the blueprint to the definitive Lipa sound. 'I was able to write about how I was feeling that very moment. Every time I listen back to the track it takes me back to that exact moment and how I felt,' she told *Noisey* in February 2016, on the eve of its release. Hearing the finished track was a big moment because she knew, finally, that she had her sound: 'The beat, the darkness, the lyrics, the pop chorus,' as she described it to the BBC. 'It's the one I would take to new producers and say, "Right, this is my sound."'

She'd felt a similar visceral reaction to 'Hotter than Hell', but this was a greater leap toward artistic maturity. 'Hotter than Hell' had been the first time she felt a song truly reflected who she was – soft but strong, sometimes uncertain but ultimately sure of herself. It gave meaning to 'dark pop', the label she'd dreamed up and been carrying around in her head. 'Last Dance', however, was the wholesale realization of how she wanted to sound, from song structure to percussion to overarching ambience. It was so 'her' that it became the sound that directed the progress of *Dua Lipa*.

In writing it, she'd allowed a swell of emotion to be her guide, much more so than she had done previously. The lyric entwines romance and homesickness, addressing itself to a new boyfriend she misses because she's far from home – she urges him to fling himself into their fledgling relationship as if it were their 'last dance'. Yet the song is really Lipa momentarily at the end of her tether – weary, missing home and wanting to sleep in her own bed. She suggests that she and the new squeeze meet up in faraway 'Cali' because she's so lonely and needs company during the long spells away from everyone she knows.

What she truly wants is to return to London, but a rendezvous in California would cheer her up in the meantime. The romantic storyline may or may not have been inspired by a real person; either way, it doesn't matter. Underlying the missing-her-boo lyric is the real story, of desperately wanting to be somewhere else. Giving in to that moment of homesickness in Toronto rather than stoically ignoring it gave Lipa a much greater understanding of what she was about.

Thanks to 'Last Dance', the *Dua Lipa* album began to progress in earnest, though due to delays it wouldn't be released until June 2017. In all, she wrote 160 songs – 148 more than would appear on the finished album. Koz, meanwhile, became a regular Lipa collaborator, producing and/or co-writing 'Levitating', 'Physical', 'IDGAF' and other canonical Lipa tracks. In 2020, she explained their working relationship on an episode of the Netflix music series *Song Exploder*: 'Koz is always my No. 1 man that I love to have in the studio.' Their closeness was such that when she started to think about *Future Nostalgia*, he was part of the tight inner circle she gathered around her — the collaborators with whom she felt most comfortable and productive. Some musicians prefer to be alone when creating, but not Lipa. Being part of a team unlocks her imagination and she only has to look at her list of hits to see the result.

Chapter 5

RARE HOMEGROWN SUCCESS

In February 2017, Lipa found herself in the happy position of having three singles in the Top 15 at the same time: 'Be the One', 'No Lie' (a feature with Sean Paul) and 'Scared to Be Lonely' (with Dutch DJ/producer Martin Garrix). It was by coincidence rather than design: 'No Lie', for instance, had been out since November but took three months to creep up the chart, while 'Be the One' had flopped upon its original release in 2015 but was rereleased in the UK at the end of 2016 because it had done well in Europe. Coincidence or not, it couldn't have come at a better time for Lipa. She was then in the final stages of putting together *Dua Lipa* and having three hits simultaneously made her seem the hottest singer of the moment – an excellent preamble to the album.

By that February, Lipa had put out or been featured on what can only be described as quite a lot of singles. Finally, with that month's triple success, things were coming to fruition. The album was around the corner, and 2017 was shaping up to be her breakthrough year after two years of slow build-up. Her first single was 'New Love', released in August 2015 to a muted reception. As mentioned previously, it didn't sell or stream enough to get into the chart, but it got plenty of 'Wow, who's *that?*' reaction from journalists and influencers. Boosted by her nomination for the Sound of 2016 award, she saw four of her next five releases – 'Be the One', 'Hotter than Hell', 'Blow Your Mind (Mwah)' and 'Scared to Be Lonely' – chart in the Top 30. The tune she wrote with Koz and Talay Riley, 'Last Dance', came out in the gap between 'Be the One' and 'Hotter Than Hell' but didn't chart.

Seven singles were released (the seventh, the Miguel collaboration 'Lost in Your Light', stalled at No. 86) before her album saw the light of day. The singles succeeded in their aim, which was to stoke excitement about *Dua Lipa*. It was scheduled for 30 September 2016 – just in time for the industry's all-important fourth-quarter sales period, which includes Christmas and traditionally sees more records sold than at any other time of year. To the chagrin of record retailers, that was changed to February 2017 – the label said it needed more time to have it ready for worldwide release – and then June 2017. The second delay, Lipa said, was to allow time 'to fit in some new songs and exciting collaborations that are in the works', but she promised it would be out on 2 June.

Part of the reason for this new postponement was that so many singles had already been released she was worried that without the aforesaid new tracks, the LP would sound like 'Dua Lipa's Greatest Hits'. The long wait was also connected with the label wanting her to break America before the album came out. At this, UK fans fretted. Some wondered why Warner's hadn't seized its chance when 'Hotter than Hell' became a big British hit in the summer of 2016. It did only moderately well in the chart – No. 15 – but was leapt on by clubs and radio, creating a buzz. The fandom thought that would have been the perfect time to release the LP in Britain; let Warner's worry about America later. Other followers were concerned about the age of some of the songs; it seemed a misjudgement to delay a record containing several tracks that had been written and mixed as far back as 2014. Either way, the concern was that the longer the wait, the greater the likelihood that she would miss her shot at stardom.

But one exceptionally prescient fan thought differently, writing on the Popheads forum in January 2017: 'This [delay] could help her a bit. If she releases a great boppy party single, she could dominate summer.' That's exactly what she did. First, though, the 'exciting collaborations' she'd teased were 'Lost in Your Light' and 'Homesick', featuring Coldplay's Chris Martin (she was a huge admirer and asked a label staffer whether it would be possible to work with him; he ended up not just co-writing the song but singing on it). Both tracks were created on hasty writing trips to Los Angeles early in 2017 – but the biggest thing to come out of those visits was 'New Rules'. When she recorded it, she loved it and expected it to do well but had no idea what it would mean to her career. This was the great boppy party single everyone had been waiting for.

The album duly arrived on 2 June and immediately streamed well. That was inevitable, given the number of hits on it. Of the twelve tracks on the standard edition, so far six had been singles and there would soon be bonus and deluxe editions of the album that contained even more. It peaked at No. 3 in Britain, No. 27 in the US.

Reviews of *Dua Lipa* were positive, though not as euphoric as they would be for *Future Nostalgia* three years later. But critics agreed that, for a first record, it was highly promising. So, although *DIY* thought 'New Rules', which wasn't yet out as a single, 'already sounds dated', the reviewer conceded that the record also contained 'bangers aplenty'. *Line of Best Fit*'s critic thought 'Homesick' was 'tacked on and unnecessary' but praised the rest of the album as 'a wholly fun trip ... with a charismatic protagonist'. *NME*'s reviewer was far less cautious: '[The album] doesn't so much hint at Dua Lipa becoming a superstar as scream it from the rooftops,' its critic said, concluding, 'She's the real deal.'

The album reached the Top 10 in countries around Europe, as well as in Australia and New Zealand. The year ended with Spotify identifying her as the most streamed female artist of 2017 in the UK and with five Brit Awards nominations, the most ever received in a single year by a female artist. For that she could thank 'New Rules'. If the song hadn't set her career on fire she would likely have received a couple of nominations, but not five. They were

British Breakthrough, British Female, British Album, British Single and British Video. At the ceremony in February 2018, she won the Breakthrough and Female gongs, a respectable tally for a first outing.

Lipa 'always knew' it was going to be 'New Rules' that made the difference, she told GQ in January 2018, reflecting on the whirlwind that had been 2017. In other words, although the album was already selling pretty well during the summer of 2017, she was aware that 'New Rules', scheduled for release on 7 July, was going to send this new era sky-high. She was right. Not only was it her first UK No. 1, and the first No. 1 by a solo female artist since Adele's 'Hello' two years earlier, it was the song that broke her to the wider public.

Suddenly, far more people knew who she was. She likened the track to rocket fuel, giving 'the push I needed globally, allowing people to really hear my album and hear my songs', she told Rolling Stone. Looking back a year later, she told ET Canada that while she had always intended to make 'New Rules' the first single after Dua Lipa came out, its supercharged ascent had shocked her. 'You can never prepare yourself for what happened to that song. It took on a complete life of its own. Obviously, it was what I wanted to happen,' she laughed, 'but I never expected it.'

Dua Lipa benefited from the track's enormous popularity to the tune of 6 million sales and 10 billion Spotify streams – the latter is the highest recorded for an album by a female artist. Those figures are the cumulative total as of late 2022, but by the end of 2017 she had already sold a healthy 1.2 million albums globally. Half of those were physical copies, proving that people were buying into Lipa as an artist. That point is important. When any track in the world can be streamed instantly, younger listeners often like particular songs but have no great interest in the artist who made them – the idea of closely following a career is alien to many. Going to the trouble of buying a CD indicates real admiration.

And the sales repaid Warner's faith in her. Few pop acts are given the freedom to develop over several years and many singles. For twenty years prior, new artists were expected to prove themselves within one or two singles or face being dropped by their label. Case in point: Girl Thing, a group conceived by a major label in the late 1990s as (they hoped) a new Spice Girls. Their first single reached a disappointing No. 8, while the label had expected it to top the charts. Still, their label A&R manager Simon Cowell (not yet famous for the *X Factor*) was confident that the 'much stronger' second single would do it. 'This is going to work for them,' he predicted. It got to No. 25 and their UK label, having spent a rumoured £1.5 million developing them, quietly dropped them.

If Lipa had been subject to the same strictures, the mediocre performance of her own first two singles ('New Love' didn't chart; 'Be the One' reached No. 9) would have led to her being 'released from her contract', as it's euphemistically known. After 'Be the One', it would be another six singles before she revisited the Top 10 – but the gap afforded crucial breathing space while she worked on her music. When 'New Rules' hit, it was obvious that it had been time well spent.

Would *Dua Lipa* have stacked up all those sales and streams without the boost of 'New Rules' and its hugely popular video? The odds are that it wouldn't have. Landing a big summer single is a pop star's dream because it provides the soundtrack to every beach party and barbecue before lodging itself in the mind as a happy memory — the reason that British holidaymakers used to come home with whatever Europop novelty had been big in the Costa del Sol discos. 'New Rules' was the cool version of the big summer song. It was everywhere throughout July and August 2017 and drove sales of the album. In that respect, it helped that it was a new song, because it made the LP more of a value-for-money buy.

Though the song itself is a very superior piece of electropop/trop house with a ferociously catchy chorus, its video was also critical to its success. There was just something 'You go, girl' about seeing Lipa and her eight 'best friends', all in pastel dressing gowns, energetically stopping her from contacting a toxic ex-boyfriend. With its racially diverse cast and emphatic girl-power theme, it was a totemic clip.

The inspiration had come from a picture Lipa kept on her phone — one of several she'd stored as potential references for the video. It showed Naomi Campbell and American model Kristen McMenamy posing together in a 1993 Gianni Versace ad. The picture, taken by Richard Avedon, was very much of its time: two supermodels elegantly convening in couture outfits. When Lipa talked about the photo in interviews while promoting the single, what she particularly remembered was that Campbell was carrying McMenamy on her back. It was actually McMenamy toting Campbell, but, either way, Lipa was struck by the idea of the women relying on each other and working together. It became a formative influence for 'New Rules' – so much so that she recreated it in the video. Three minutes and thirty-three seconds in, she and seven of the eight dancers pair off into piggybacking couples. Lipa is one of the lifters, effortlessly hoisting a dancer onto her back – and on a fashion note, all the lifters and liftees accomplish this while wearing stiletto heels.

The evident bond between Lipa and the dancers was such that she was asked by an interviewer whether they were all friends in real life. No, she said; she hadn't known them before, but they spent the entire time in each other's company and even took their breaks together during the two days' rehearsal plus filming time. The atmosphere had been 'lovely', she remembered, which was clear from their on-screen chemistry. In her offstage life, her real best friends played a similarly supportive role: 'They're the people who will talk me out of anything crazy.'

The video also owed something to the visual for Beyoncé's 2016 single 'Formation', which foregrounded the idea of strong female friendships and showed scenes of a long row of women bending and stretching in sync, with Beyoncé in the middle. The subject of that video – Black culture and activism – was some way removed from that of 'New Rules', but in both, the sight of women uniting in unbreakable solidarity was unmistakeable and impressive.

It could be said, in fact, that the video was the difference between 'New Rules' being merely a big hit and being a blockbuster. Suddenly, other female singers were making contact – Zara Larsson loved it; Lorde said it was one of the best videos she'd seen; Tegan and Sara tweeted that it was 'so so so great'; Camila Cabello exclaimed, 'So sick dua!!!!' It was such an across-the-board sensation that when Selena Gomez was considering returning to former boyfriend Justin Bieber, her disapproving fans sent her memes and links to the song. By 2022, it had accrued 2.7 billion views.

Ironically, on 21 July, a fortnight after 'New Rules' came out, the *Guardian* ran a long article about the marked lack of female artists breaking through pop's glass ceiling. Nineteen young singers were mentioned, of whom only two – Lipa and Billie Eilish – were on their way to major stardom. Others on the list, such as Zara Larsson and Anne-Marie, went on to find reasonable success, but most, including Halsey, Raye and Sigrid (despite winning the BBC Music Sound of 2018 poll), couldn't make much headway.

(Note: five years after the article was written, pop's upper reaches are still populated by those who were there before – Rihanna, Grande, Swift – along with incomers like Lipa and Eilish and one or two newer names whose stars are ascending so quickly that they seem destined to reach the top tier. Doja Cat and Blackpink rapper Lisa, who was the most searched-for female artist of April 2022, look like contenders, but compared to the lengthy list of male success stories, women are barely scratching the surface.)

The *Guardian* quoted veteran music publicist Ruth Drake, who said, 'Pop music is not being led by any female pop star right at this minute.' The article contended that to get a foothold, let alone reach the top, female singers had to cover multiple bases in a way that men didn't. They were expected to be politically and socially aware when interviewed by broadsheets, musically knowledgeable when speaking to the music press 'and urbane and edgy for the arty fashion magazines'. Getting the attention of the fashion sector was an essential box to tick because pop stars who are seen as fashion-forward attract brand sponsorships.

By then, Lipa had ticked every one of those boxes, including the urbane-and-edgy requirement. Thanks to her 'edginess' – translation: she listened to cool music and wore cool clothes – in May 2017 she had been invited to collaborate with Foot Locker on a series of ads that showed her modelling the chain's trainers. Another set of adverts appeared in November, featuring her in a newly unveiled collection that included the Vans Old Skool Platform Sherpa and the Adidas Superstar Fur. The agency that put together the campaign, FRUKT, chose Lipa because of her 'pan-European appeal [and] young millennial audience, and combined social reach of 2.24 million', which would increase to nearly 88 million on Instagram alone by early 2023. A report written at the end of 2017 noted that Foot Locker had signed the deal at exactly the right time, before her album came out; when *Dua Lipa* did appear, along with 'New Rules', the brand could congratulate itself that the hottest singer in pop was advertising its trainers. Lipa told the style magazine *Grazia*: 'Foot Locker has my back when it comes to streetwear and sneakers.'

She's since endorsed Puma trainers with two collections of her own designs and promoted Truly Hard Seltzer, Pepe Jeans and the Yves Saint Laurent perfume Libre. She appeared in advertising for Versace's Fall–Winter 2021 campaign – strikingly tall and glamorous, she modelled short dresses in primary colours and handbags priced at £1,620. Then there was the witty 2022 Evian campaign, titled Drink True. She appeared in a series of ads, one of which brought her together with Emma Raducanu. The seventy-five-second clip, called 'Skill Swap', had Dua and the tennis star giving each other a how-to lesson.

Girl power at its funniest, it's worth describing: Lipa's 'Physical' is the soundtrack as Raducanu tries to perfect Lipa's forehand ('"Perfect" is quite ambitious,' Lipa says); in return, Lipa teaches Raducanu how to dance. Even when Raducanu shows her how to grip the racket, turn from the shoulders and swing, Lipa proves no budding Wimbledon champ. 'When do we do the noise?' she asks. 'What noise?' replies Raducanu. Lipa emitted a Maria Sharapova-like 'HUH!' 'Optional,' says Raducanu. She turns out to be a better dancer than Lipa is a tennis player, though she might have an unfair advantage – one of the dances Lipa demonstrates is the hip-twisting shimmy that inspired dozens of memes at her expense in 2018. That was before she took instruction from choreographer Charm La'donna and became a skilled mover (more on this later). For Evian, she brings back the viral dance, and the innately rhythmic Raducanu picks up the steps immediately. The ad ends with the two racing off set with a trolleyful of pink Evian-logoed tennis balls.

There have also been tie-ins with Johnnie Walker scotch, Jaguar and MAC cosmetics. The last of those produced a shade of pearly lipgloss named after her, a new addition to MAC's well-established Cremesheen Glass range. At £18, a tube of Dua Lipa Cremesheen was an affordable, appealing way to identify with her, and the marketing was subtle and well thought out. It was spearheaded by a TV commercial titled 'Future Forward' that, apart from a discreet MAC logo flashing up at the start, didn't seem like a commercial at all but rather a female-empowerment video. To the tune of 'Hotter than Hell', it followed Lipa into a male boxing gym, where she got into the ring with a muscled opponent and, of course, walloped him. 'Being strong is beautiful,' she said in the voiceover. Knowing Lipa's perfectionism, she probably trained for days to make the boxing sequence realistic. Premiered in May 2017, it was another building block in the promotional campaign leading to *Dua Lipa*'s release.

But not every brand was an obvious fit with her Gen Z constituency – a Jaguar, for instance, is beyond the reach of most fans. Yet it's advantageous for brands to be affiliated with a pop star who is perceived as hip and genuine, and the car endorsed by Lipa, the electric Jaguar I-PACE (starting price in 2022: £65,780), had a hook designed to capture Gen Z's interest. When it came on the market in late 2018, it was accompanied by a website that invited I-PACE owners to remix a Lipa song. It was one of those concepts that was harder to explain than to do: the website responded to an individual's style of driving; and whatever music the driver listened to most on Spotify was 'remixed' by the site so tracks became the driver's own version.

But the site also offered a previously unreleased Lipa song,

'Want To', which had been made for *Dua Lipa* but ended up unused until the I-PACE link-up. 'Every fan can create their own remix,' Lipa said. 'I love to push boundaries with my music ... it's a hi-tech project combining music and Jaguar technology.' According to Jaguar's brand experience agency Imagination, somewhere north of 90,000 remixes have been created.

During the *Dua Lipa* promotional cycle, which ran from early 2017 to late 2019, when singles began to emerge from the upcoming *Future Nostalgia*, Lipa's value as a brand ambassador rocketed. Influencer Intelligence, a marketing and data platform, analysed her appeal in February 2019, when her Pepe Jeans collection launched. It determined that her audience see her first as 'desirable', someone who seems stylish and sophisticated, then as 'charming' and 'confident'. Her 'awareness' score – the amount of online conversation about her – is high at nearly seventy. It made her a good choice for a fashion brand like Pepe. The analysis concluded that Pepe could have opted for an edgier campaign by using a 'disruptive influencer', but by teaming up with someone who's already known and liked by the brand's demographic, Pepe would broaden its appeal.

On 2 June 2022, the fifth anniversary of *Dua Lipa*'s release, the singer looked back on a tumultuous half-decade. Writing on social media, she said, 'I'm so proud of every baby step and stepping stone, every room, club and venue, every artist, songwriter and producer I've been lucky to collaborate with ...' It's an unusual pop star who remembers to thank the people who've helped them on the way up, but it's part of her 'be nice' credo.

At the end of 2017, she had reason to count her blessings. In June, she'd played Glastonbury for the second time. She'd first done it in 2016 on the John Peel Stage, but that brief set was nothing like this one; she performed on the Peel Stage again, but this time in front of a capacity crowd, with those who couldn't get into the tent crowding outside in the rain. Their enthusiasm took her breath away. She'd been worried that nobody would turn up – shortly before her set the tent was still nearly empty and she tried to convince herself she didn't care.

When she ran onto the stage ten minutes later, she found a packed and cheering house. 'Oh, man. So many people here,' she marvelled. 'Thank you so much.' Just before the last song, wreathed in smiles, she added, 'You're really making my dreams come true. Thank you, thank you, thank you for coming.' With that, she dove into 'Be the One'. Impulsively climbing on top of the crowd-control barrier, she stood there – two security staff clutched her legs so she wouldn't topple into the audience – and had the visceral thrill of everyone in the tent singing with her. It was an unforgettable moment.

Backstage after her set, she told *NME* that it had been 'my favourite [performance] by far'. Ed Sheeran was one of that year's headliners, and Lipa mused that she'd love to collaborate with him, which gives an idea of the extent of her ambition and fearlessness. In 2017, Sheeran was one of the UK's few bona fide pop superstars and was deemed deeply uncool by hipsters for his emollient tunefulness. Dua, who was considered very cool and had just one album to her name, didn't perceive a divide between

Sheeran and herself — he was just a musician she thought would be an interesting collaboration partner. It hasn't happened yet, but since that day she has caught up with him in one respect: as previously mentioned, her 'Levitating' and his 'Bad Habits' were the most played tracks of 2021 in Amazon warehouses in Britain.

Other than Sheeran, Adele and Harry Styles, the UK hasn't produced many world-beating pop artists in the past decade. Lipa is an exception — what the *Guardian* called 'a rare homegrown success' who commands the same devotion in Buenos Aires as she does in Birmingham. In an article titled 'How Dua Lipa became the most streamed woman of 2017', that paper's Laura Snapes suggested that the reason she had done so well in the UK that year was that she represented the 'authentic voice of young British womanhood: independent, cool and in command of her own sexuality'.

And the fact that her route to the top was 'organic' shouldn't be underestimated. By taking time to mature as an artist while also putting out music regularly, she attracted fans who appreciated her authenticity — in 'Hotter than Hell', she'd boasted that she was the 'realest'. Realness — being herself both on stage and off — was an attractive quality that made girls and young women want to share her journey. Warner's and TaP Management exerted a light touch on their end, making the Lipa movement feel less like a 'campaign' and more like serendipity.

The *Guardian* story was greeted sceptically by many readers, if the comments underneath were any guide. Some flatly declared that she owed her success to Auto-Tune pitch-correcting software (she doesn't use it). Others scoffed that she was fine but hardly in the Beatles' league (a false equivalence; she wasn't trying to compete with the Beatles), and a few claimed ignorance altogether ('Never heard of her. Is she famous in popular culture?'). One person mused, 'I suppose the acid test will be asking about Dua Lipa in December 2018.'

Presumably, they would have had a shock if they could have looked forward to November 2022, when *Heat* published its annual '30 Richest Celebrities Under 30' list. Lipa, who had never previously been on it, was No. 2 with, the magazine estimated, £69 million in the bank – only Styles was richer, with £116 million. *Heat* said her money came from a variety of sources: the Future Nostalgia tour, product endorsements, the 5 million tickets sold for her November 2020 livestream concert Studio 2054, a rumoured role in an upcoming Barbie movie, and an investment in female-run hair and beauty brand Dizziak. The company's website has a banner at the top saying 'Welcome to Dizziak Dua Lipa', while Lipa has said, 'Dizziak is in a category all of their own and I'm thrilled to be an investor in their journey.' Sixty-nine million is a staggering sum, and she's worked for it; her Instagram might brim with snaps of her wearing bogglingly expensive clothes in palm-fringed holiday retreats, but, equally, there are plenty of pictures of her earning the money, on stage and in studio sessions that run late into the night.

She spent much of 2017 on tour, both as headliner and support act. Headline dates took place in mid-sized venues, but in America, opening for Bruno Mars at ten shows on his 24K Magic tour, she discovered how it felt to play the country's largest arenas.

There was more big-stage experience in February and March 2018, when she supported Mars at fourteen shows in Australia and New Zealand. She'd been booked for the entire Oceania leg – eighteen shows – but had to drop out of four when her wisdom teeth needed immediate removal while she was in Brisbane.

The dental problem occasioned her first Twitter spat – a rite of passage for pop stars, who can't consider themselves true celebrities until they've been embroiled in an exchange of words on social media. While Lipa was on bed rest in Australia, still recovering from surgery, she made an appearance on the *Jimmy Kimmel Live!* talk show, singing her new single, 'IDGAF'. It had been pre-recorded in Los Angeles in February but was broadcast on one of the nights she was supposed to be opening for Mars. An entertainment reporter on Australia's *Today* show, Richard Wilkins, waspishly suggested that she hadn't cancelled the date because of her teeth but had actually flown to California to do Kimmel's show. A moment's consideration would have shown that the logistics were impossible: it's a thirteen-hour flight each way, and Lipa would have had to race to Kimmel's studio, perform the song and head straight back to Australia.

Annoyed and in pain, she tweeted, 'If you were a good journalist you would've done proper research instead of talking out of your ass. *Jimmy Kimmel* was shot in Feb in LA and aired yesterday.' She attached a photo of her swollen mouth (both tweet and photo have since been deleted). A chastened Wilkins tweeted back: 'Sincere apologies. Didn't mean to misinform. Your fans and my son have severely castigated me!' But he took the apology a step further. On *Today* the next morning, he referred to Lipa's tweet – 'She told me I was talking out of my backside' – then rose from his seat, turned around and displayed his backside, which had a white card stuck to it. 'Sorry,' it said.

Dua might not have remembered that she had greatly impressed Wilkins while she was in Australia in April 2016, promoting 'Be the One' (it was an iTunes Top 5 hit there) and arranging dates there for that July. He interviewed her and afterward wrote on Facebook: 'This young lady Dua Lipa is going to be a HUGE star!' Alongside was a photo of them, both smiling.

Dua didn't respond to Wilkins's backside apology, and the matter seemed to be closed. She didn't play in Australia again until late 2022, when the Future Nostalgia tour finished its long round-the-world run with nine Antipodean dates (the finale was in the Albanian capital Tirana, on 28 November). On the 2022 visit, she played the same venues she had when opening for Bruno Mars – Melbourne's Rod Laver Arena and the Qudos Bank Arena in Sydney among them – but this time as headliner. Three days before the arena dates started, Lipa staged a special 'intimate' show in the Melbourne suburb St Kilda. As if to illustrate how spectacularly her star had risen since 2018, there were 25,000 applications for the 2,800 tickets. It was, said the *Sydney Morning Herald*, 'one of the most memorable and joyous pop shows of the year', and the *Guardian*, after wondering why the show hadn't taken place 'out in the regions', which rarely host stars of this magnitude, pronounced her 'irresistible'. The latter reviewer also made the astute observation that Lipa is wasted on small theatre venues where fans aren't allowed to dance – to be properly appreciated, she needs to be seen 'in her element in a big stadium'.

Right there was the clearest possible verification of her standing. Only a few pop artists are at their best in stadiums – U2's Bono, who's one of them, began a speech at the 2004 UK Labour Party conference with: 'Excuse me if I appear a little nervous. I'm not used to appearing before crowds of less than 80,000 people.' Lipa is also one of them. On the Latin American leg of Future Nostalgia, she played to 100,000 people over two nights in Argentina, 65,000 in one night in Mexico City – the largest crowd she had ever drawn before the Tirana show, when 200,000 people saw her. She was assuredly in her element, writing the day after Mexico City, '*Que locura!* Living on a cloud!' It doesn't get bigger than that.

Back in 2017, after finishing her American support slot with Bruno Mars, she spent the rest of the year on stages around the world, including four shows with Coldplay on the Latin American stretch of their A Head Full of Dreams tour. The audience-count at those concerts dwarfed Mars's by a considerable way – on Lipa's first night, on 8 November at Allianz Parque in São Paulo, she performed for 48,000 people, and for similar numbers at the other gigs. Her ten-song setlist didn't include 'Homesick', the song co-written by Chris Martin, but Coldplay's set featured 'Everglow', a piano-led ballad that many Lipa and Coldplay fans consider similar to 'Homesick'. There *is* an undeniable likeness, even if it's only the fact that both tunes pivot on the same delicate sense of loss.

While in South America, she found time between Coldplay dates to slip in solo shows in São Paulo and Buenos Aires. Martin joined her on stage at the first, a 9 November headliner at Audio Club, and the pair dueted on an encore of 'Homesick'. It was a rather bumpy version, with Martin missing a couple of piano notes and signalling to Lipa to start the song again. The audience, delighted at the show of fallibility, cheered him on with real affection.

At the end of that year, manager Ben Mawson summed things up with: 'She's very happy with her success, but very keen to build on it in 2018.' She did, and then some. The *Guardian* reader who had thought she would slip into obscurity within a year – 'I suppose the acid test will be asking about Dua Lipa in December 2018' – would have to eat their words.

Chapter 6

ONE KISS

By December 2018, even those who claimed they'd never heard of Lipa had a hard time avoiding her. Departing from her usual course of releasing multiple singles each year, in 2018 she put out only three. But two of them — 'IDGAF' and 'One Kiss' — were smashes, with both nominated in the British Single of the Year category at the 2019 Brit Awards, and 'One Kiss' winning it. The third, 'Electricity', which reached a respectable UK No. 4, was somewhat overshadowed by the other two, probably due to its being a collaboration with Silk City rather than a solo single. Nevertheless, it won the 2019 Grammy for Best Dance Recording — and Lipa was named Best New Artist at the same ceremony.

It's a slight to call 'One Kiss' a mere 'smash'. It's more accurate to say that it was 'a route one smasheroo', in the words of critic Graeme Virtue. It was a standalone single, made with Calvin Harris and not included on *Dua Lipa* (it was added to the late-2018 reissue, *Dua Lipa: Complete Edition*), making it the first 'new' music she'd released in some time. It spent eight weeks at the top of the UK singles chart in the summer of 2018 – a deluxe tropical house embodiment of the perfect summer song, much as 'New Rules' was the previous year. The best-selling single of 2018 in the UK, 'One Kiss' won British Single of the Year at the 2019 Brit Awards, and its video, starring Harris as an impassive poolside waiter and Lipa as a fantastically imperious tropical glamour girl, was MTV's most played of 2018.

Before that, though, was 'IDGAF' ('I Don't Give a Fuck'). The last word is said on the record, and although the radio edit cuts it out, its absence is scarcely noticeable in a song laden with 'gang vocals' – a term for a squad of people stridently singing all or part of a song; in this case, the gang was Dua's multi-tracked own voice. The song's release was held back for a while to let the previous single, 'New Rules', play itself out in the chart; it finally appeared in January 2018, a full six months after 'New Rules' came out – one of the longest gaps between Dua singles. It was the last *Dua Lipa* track to become a single, and as a creative decision it felt right to stop there. The album and its various reissues had together yielded eight singles, and to release more would have involved using material that wasn't strong enough on its own.

There was also a need to draw a line under the *Dua Lipa* era and start thinking about the future – she began to write the second album early in 2018, a process that would take the better part of two years. On top of that, she had to reckon with her new status since the success of 'New Rules'. That song and its video were such a strong package that it turned her into a proper A-list contender, or she was at least on 'the periphery of the pop A-list', said Popjustice, taking the cautious view. All this militated against using another single from *Dua Lipa*. To this day, some fans feel hard done by because this song or that song wasn't a standalone, but Lipa and her team made the right call.

In short, 'IDGAF' signalled a goodbye to Lipa's first 'era'. The second wouldn't properly begin until the end of 2019, when the early fruits of *Future Nostalgia* surfaced in the shape of the single 'Don't Start Now'. In August 2018, Lipa herself mused that *Dua Lipa*'s cycle was coming to an end; the line in the sand would be 30 September, when she finished her Self-Titled tour (as it was known). Therefore, the period roughly encompassing spring 2018 to autumn 2019 can be seen as a transition from the *Dua Lipa* era to the *Future Nostalgia* one.

The transition was personal as well as musical. With her profile rising throughout 2018 due to the one-two punch of 'IDGAF' and 'One Kiss', Lipa evolved into a more 'conscious' pop star. She had been politically and culturally literate almost since childhood, but now, capturing the attention of an increasingly large audience, she began to see the world differently. Her perception of her place in the world would broaden during 2018 — she was now aware of the power that was increasingly at her disposal and used it to denounce, for instance, the ingrained sexism of the Grammy Awards and to support LGBT rights.

But she also became increasingly focused. Now that people were listening to her opinions as well as her music, she grew skilled at choosing the right time and place to express them. Her greatest moment so far of whisking together activism and pop stardom would come well into the *Future Nostalgia* era, at the 2021 Brit Awards, where she won British Album of the Year and British Female Solo Artist. Collecting the trophy for the latter, she addressed the audience, which was comprised not just of industry staff and nominated artists but 2,500 key workers. (The ceremony, held at London's O2 Arena in May of that year—three months later than usual because of Covid restrictions — was closely watched by both the government and the public, as it was a test event to determine the viability of large gatherings taking place without social distancing.)

Each winning artist was given two trophies: a large multicoloured statuette and a smaller silver-coated one, the latter intended to be given to someone the winner considered worthy as 'an act of kindness'. Lipa's choice for the silver statue was Dame Elizabeth Anionwu, Emeritus Professor of Nursing at the University of West London. Lipa made a fiery acceptance speech that began with thank-yous to her team and worked its way up to an impassioned demand for frontline workers to receive better pay for their efforts throughout the pandemic. She quoted Dame Elizabeth, who had spent much of her career working with people living with sickle-cell disease and thalassaemia: 'There's a massive disparity between gratitude and respect for frontline workers.' Referring to the lockdown custom of standing on the front doorstep every Thursday evening and applauding for two minutes, Lipa continued, 'It's very good to clap for them, but we need to pay them.' She urged the crowd to unite in a round of applause that would 'give Boris [Johnson, then Prime Minister] a message that we all support a fair pay rise for our frontline'.

She knew it would get attention; every media outlet duly quoted her, and the simmering issue of pay increases for staff working with Covid patients heated up once again.

Returning to 2018 and 'IDGAF', there was evidence on the single sleeve that Lipa was changing and, indeed, didn't give a fuck. The slightly fuzzy cover photo showed her standing in front of a mirror in a backstage loo in Antwerp, wearing a bra and shaving her right underarm as she got ready for a show. It was an everyday pre-gig chore that, in this context, was also intimate because it offered a glimpse of her offstage self. Lipa decided to use this unglamorous shot for the cover of 'IDGAF' because she was learning to be, and to show, her authentic self. Not everyone liked the picture: a fan tweeted, 'What kind of cover is this? I don't like it.' 'Why not?' he was asked. 'It is really weird. Who does a cover in a bathroom?' Perhaps Lipa was hoping fans like him would examine his own response to it – that would justify her having used it.

The writer of 'IDGAF' was UK singer and songwriter MNEK, who created it from his perspective. When Lipa heard the song, she added lyrics to reflect her own experience of pushing away a cheating ex-partner who was trying to get back into her life. A year after it became Lipa's first hit of 2018, MNEK reflected on Facebook: 'When a song I've written for another artist does well, the question people ask me is "Why didn't you keep that for yourself?"' The reason, he said, was altruism. When another musician recorded one of his songs, they were using it to express something of themselves, and he had helped them to do it. And it was still his song – he could always perform it at his own shows, so it was win-win.

The song was put together in Los Angeles on the same quick-turnaround writing trip that produced 'Homesick', her duet with Chris Martin. It was one of the last songs written for *Dua Lipa*, and due to the aforementioned gang vocals it's a pugnacious piece of music that's akin to having a group of girls shouting (rhythmically) in your ear.

The best version of it isn't the recorded one on the album but a Radio 1 Live Lounge performance that took place in February 2018, shortly after the song was released. The video of the occasion is on YouTube and well worth watching. Lipa had put together a multinational female supergroup to back her – fellow Brit Charli XCX, Sweden's Zara Larsson, Danish singer-songwriter MØ and Finnish vocalist Alma – and between them they did right by the song. With Dua standing at the front and the others lined up behind her, they looked like a hipster Spice Girls and sang like a squad of righteous avengers. The F-word in the title couldn't be sung; when they reached it in the chorus, there was a brief silence and Lipa smirked at the camera. Her expression spoke volumes. Harmonizing powerfully, the five were indomitable together. If the 'boy' they addressed in the song – a real person from Dua's past – chanced to hear the song, and he could hardly miss it given that it reached No. 3 and spent twenty-nine weeks in the chart, he would be under no illusions about Dua's feelings. She really didn't give a fuck.

Lipa's lyric sprang from a text she received from this ex-boyfriend. He'd hurt her deeply, having been caught 'creeping' (coming on to another girl) by a friend of hers. Now, all of a sudden, he wanted to say hello. 'How dare he?' she thought. He made such a mess of things and now he was telling her he missed her? Maybe he was crawling back because in the interim she'd become a pop star and that suddenly made her irresistible? That's the gist of the song, and while she has said that parts of the storyline are fictionalized, it's obvious from the vehemence in her vocal that most of it is fundamentally true.

Together with its striking video, which pitted two Dua Lipas against each other – one, dressed in purple, represented her stronger side; the other, in orange, her more sensitive self–'IDGAF' was thematically akin to 'New Rules' (which was written on that same trip to Los Angeles). Backed by two teams of dancers also wearing purple or orange, the Duas ultimately find a rapport. Just as Lipa's girlfriends made her see the light in the 'New Rules' clip, the two warring Duas eventually agree that the most important love is self-love.

And, as with 'New Rules', it was a song that was greatly enhanced by its video. Heard on its own, it was a storming get-out-of-my-life track, but in tandem with the video – which took twenty-two hours to shoot, so complex were its interpretive dance routines – it's a double whammy. Most reviewers agreed that 'IDGAF' was, in the perceptive opinion of The 405, 'a stadium stormer' – the kind of thing that prompts mass singalongs and fists pumping the air. Only *Line of Best Fit*'s reviewer was less keen, feeling unmoved by Lipa's proclamation that she DGAF. She sounded like 'she's convincing herself she doesn't care', making the song 'fall a little flat'. That didn't stop it being awarded platinum discs for 1.2 million and 2 million 'track-equivalent sales' in Britain and America, respectively.

Just three months after 'IDGAF', in April came 'One Kiss', still her longest running No. 1 single to this day. It bedded in at the top for eight weeks starting 26 April and was the UK's biggest single of 2018. It also won the Brit Award for British Single of the Year. It was, in just about every way, massive. It was even adopted by Liverpool FC fans. After Lipa performed the song at the 2018 Champions League final in Kyiv, Ukraine, where Liverpool were bested by Real Madrid, 'One Kiss' became a Reds supporters' anthem. They sing it at trophy celebrations and home games, where it vies with 'You'll Never Walk Alone' as their definitive tune.

Lipa and Harris had met, briefly, in 2015, when she was promoting 'Be the One', a song he loved. From that point she was on his radar, and after a couple of years had passed he found an old song he'd started making and realized it could be perfect for her. He sent it to her in January 2018 via Twitter direct message – and she didn't reply for two weeks. When she did get in touch, she told him she'd heard it 'and didn't get it'. He asked her to listen again, and the second time 'she got it', he recounted later. That was lucky for both of them. 'She changed quite a few bits,' he added.

When he approached her, she was at Geejam Studios in Jamaica, working on material for the next album, but she was going to LA afterward for a show at the Palladium, so their schedules meshed. Even if she hadn't had to be in Los Angeles, she would have gone just for this opportunity. She'd spent months telling interviewers that she'd love to work with Harris, the most successful producer/DJ of his generation (he reportedly earns around £330,000 for every DJ set he plays). She met him at his Benedict Canyon 'house–studio thing' – a place Harris describes as 'quite dark' because heavy-duty soundproofing blocks the windows and the only natural daylight comes from a skylight. The pair tossed ideas around while watching the video for a track Harris had just finished working on ('Nuh Ready Nuh Ready' featuring PartyNextDoor).

Before Lipa got involved, Harris had called in Canadian singer-songwriter Jessie Reyez, who had sung on his 2017 album *Funk Wav Bounces Vol. 1*. He asked her to come up with lyrics for the track, and what was meant to be a one-day writing session turned into a week. When Lipa arrived, 'we started rewriting it, and he was open to my ideas', she told *ET Canada*. He was willing to change things she felt strongly about and let her run with ideas. Between her ideas and what Reyez had already written, she and Harris came up with the polar opposite of the scornful 'IDGAF'. This new creation fizzed with desire, capturing the instant attraction Dua felt when the right person came onto her radar. The word 'possibilities' is repeated almost as a mantra, her voice dizzy with longing. The garage/house/EDM backing overflows with optimism.

In short, it was 'engineered to get stuck in your head', said one critic. In Britain, it amassed more 'track units' (a measure of downloads and streams together) in its first week than any previous 2018 chart-topper, including the first week of 'Nice for What', the wildly popular Drake song it replaced at No. 1. Incidentally, Drake is another artist Lipa wants to work with. It hasn't happened yet, but when she covered another of his giant hits, 'One Dance', at the 2016 Capital FM Jingle Bell Ball, she got the phrasing and rhythm just right.

Still, Calvin Harris disputed the idea that a hit could be 'engineered' during an interview on Kiss FM on 24 April, two days before 'One Kiss' topped the chart. 'You never know' when you've made a hit song, he told the Kiss crew. 'There are so many variables that can make it a hit or not a hit or a slightly bigger or smaller hit.' As if to reinforce that view, an early review of the song in *Forbes* said, 'It's hard to say that it has true hit potential upon first listen.' But Harris was just putting on a show of modesty during the Kiss interview.

Yet he has also had his disappointments: for every huge hit he's worked on, there's another that didn't meet commercial expectations. 'Nuh Ready Nuh Ready', for example, peaked in the UK at No. 48. So, if there was any way to 'engineer' a song into a guaranteed hit, he of all people would know it. Another, perhaps more accurate, theory about 'One Kiss's grip on the No. 1 spot was posited by *Fader* podcaster Matt Chandler, who reckoned that 'One Kiss' became the song of 2018 simply because it was 'palatable'. Palatability is a pretty bland marker of success, especially when it concerns a big, sparkling tune like this, but the podcast went on to say, 'It goes in your ears and you're, like, "Ooh, Dua Lipa is with me, I'm good, girl."' That's as useful an explanation as any.

Other critics were more effusive: MTV called it 'the year's first bona fide sunshine banger'; *NME* proclaimed it 'the song of the summer'; and in *The Edge*'s opinion it was 'intensely catchy', though the magazine wondered why it 'rumbled on' for 3.5 minutes when it would have been far better cut by a minute. Its appeal was so across-the-board that the worst any reviewer could muster was that it 'doesn't quite reach the quietly euphoric heights' of several tracks on *Funk Wav Bounces Vol. 1*.

Harris's comment about not being able to predict hits was exemplified by his second team-up with Lipa, the 2022 single 'Potion'. A very likeable helping of breezy synth-funk, it came out in May – just in time to jump onto summer playlists – and featured a verse from star MC Young Thug. Thus, it contained all the components of a big song – except, perhaps, palatability. It got only as far as No. 16 in the UK, which might have been a message from listeners who felt they'd had enough of the overworked DJ + female vocal + rap feature formula.

Later in 2022, while promoting his new album *Funk Wav Bounces Vol. 2*, which features 'Potion', Harris told Radio 2 presenter Zoe Ball that he rarely works with an artist more than once. Ball had asked whether he and Lipa would do a hat-trick, and his rather surprising answer was: 'As a rule, it's just the one. I actually wouldn't have [usually] done a second.' As for a third? 'Probably a third would be pushing it.' That's Harris's way of operating and doesn't impugn his friendship with Lipa, which remains solid.

As 2018 ended, Lipa made a salient observation to CNN's Becky Anderson: 'Every time I say I'm slowing down a bit, I'm not, really, because I haven't stopped at all.' She ticked off what she'd been doing, starting with the Brit Awards back in February. She'd performed at the ceremony and picked up two awards: British Breakthrough and British Female. She'd also made a sweet, apparently spontaneous gesture: when her name was read out as Breakthrough winner, she rose from her table near the stage at the O2 Arena, where she was seated with her family, and took her younger siblings by the hand, bringing them up to the stage. 'My little brother and sister probably think I'm crazy that I've just brought them up on stage with me,' she said, her eyes wet, 'but ... at the bottom of my album I thanked everyone and told them to believe in magic because it's real. And this is the closest I've come to it, so I wanted them to experience it first-hand.'

What else did she do in 2018? There was a world tour, which began in January, finished at the end of September and visited four continents. She'd made videos and travelled almost constantly. It had been a whirlwind. Her last project of 2018 was a song for the soundtrack for an upcoming manga-inspired sci-fi thriller, *Alita: Battle Angel*. It was Lipa's second movie song, the first having been 'High' for the 2018 erotic thriller *Fifty Shades Freed*, the final part of the *Fifty Shades of Grey* trilogy. This *Alita* track, 'Swan Song', had been right up her street; as soon as she saw a trailer for the film, which starred Rosa Salazar and Christoph Waltz, she felt drawn to the Alita character and wanted to be involved. Alita was not only a kick-ass cyborg, she was on a quest to mature and develop and help others.

'I relate to that, a lot. We have to speak up against the injustices of the world,' Lipa said. 'Being able to put that in a song that was really strong lyrically means so much more than your standard pop song.' Her hope was that listeners would find something of themselves in Alita and 'Swan Song'. The track was a motivational, climb-that-mountain electropopper that came with a must-see video: Lipa and dancers inhabit a ravaged future planet and Alita herself teaches Lipa martial arts moves until she acquires cyborg arms of her own. Wanting to make the scene look as natural as possible, Lipa insisted on being instructed by a martial arts expert working on the movie. She was by then engrossed in writing *Future Nostalgia*, and after a full day in the studio she spent several hours each night practising her fighting moves. It was worth the effort: the video is gripping. Having said that, the track, released in January 2019, was one of her handful of underperformers, reaching only No. 24 in the UK chart. That was probably because it came out during the industry's traditionally fallow time of year, and as an unexpected release, unconnected to an album, it was overlooked.

That was the last music she released until November of that year – a ten-month gap while she concentrated her energies on finishing *Future Nostalgia*. She'd spent most of 2018 working on it, and that would continue through 2019. The new album had been continuously on her mind almost since *Dua Lipa*'s release, and she was intent on making it as remarkable as she could. To that end, around the close of 2017 she'd spent a week working with Max Martin, the Swedish pop czar who's written smashes for — among dozens of others — Taylor Swift, Adele and Lipa's beloved P!nk. She discovered that teaming up with the most prolific pop producer of the late twentieth century didn't necessarily guarantee that they'd create a string of titanic hits. She found his methodology intriguing but antithetical to hers; he approached songwriting 'theoretically', she said. For instance, he counselled against using the same word too often in a lyric, and if he felt that a melody needed changing, he listened to it repeatedly before altering a single note. Lipa's own approach is more spontaneous, though she took on board much of his advice. The songs they wrote together haven't been released.

She'd learned something from the frenetic schedule she'd kept during the past few years, while making and then promoting *Dua Lipa*. As she toiled over *Future Nostalgia*, she concocted a game plan.

While conceiving the debut LP, Lipa was kept so busy doing touring, promo and TV that she had to write much of the record on the road, in the intervals between other commitments. There was never time to sit and breathe, let alone rehearse for gigs and television appearances, and she felt the lack of rehearsal time keenly. Perfectionist that she is, she couldn't stand walking onto a stage and feeling she hadn't been able to tweak her performance into shape. So, when it came to creating *Future Nostalgia*, she knew absolutely what she needed.

Speaking to MTV just before *FN*'s release, she revealed that she had insisted on finishing the record before planning the visual and creative sides, and she'd also taken her time about deciding how the Future Nostalgia tour might look. Before, she'd had to do all the planning and rehearsing on the hoof. 'I want to make sure that [for] every performance I do I have enough rehearsal time to be able to put on a unique performance every time, even if it is the same song,' she told MTV in early 2020. Just getting that under control would give her one less thing to worry about and free up mental space for the LP-writing task.

It was plain that she had scrupulously rehearsed her scene-stealing duet with American singer/avant-rocker Annie 'St Vincent' Clark at the 2019 Grammys – or had she? She won the Best New Artist and Best Dance Recording (for 'Electricity') categories that night, but that almost paled into insignificance compared to their 'fucked-up and sexy' (St Vincent's words) meeting of minds. It turned out that their sultry mash-up of St Vincent's 'Masseduction' and Lipa's 'One Kiss', sung with many sidelong glances at each other, was a late addition to the show, when rehearsal time was at a minimum. Yet Lipa was now such an expert performer that she pulled it off without a hitch.

As for the awards she took home from the Staples Center in Los Angeles that night, the Best New Artist gong is sometimes thought of as a poisoned chalice because of the number of winners who never fulfilled their potential, from New York pop-rockers Fun to famous non-singers Milli Vanilli, but Lipa has more than risen to the occasion. In any case, 'new' artist is a misnomer – as the only Brit nominated in the category, she may have been new in the eyes of the Grammy voting panel, but in the UK and much of the rest of the world she was already on the verge of top-tier stardom. Proof: Madame Tussauds London, the flagship location of the chain of waxworks museums, put a 'Dua Lipa' on display in February 2019 and later added new figures of her to the New York, Sydney and Amsterdam museums. What more proof is needed?

It was scant wonder that, at a gig in Mumbai in November of that year, Katy Perry stopped her show for a moment to praise that night's support act—Dua Lipa. Perry asked whether the crowd had enjoyed Lipa's set. Affirmative shrieks answered that question. 'I have a crush on Dua Lipa,' Perry went on, in the manner of someone confiding a secret. 'Make some noise if you also have a crush on Dua Lipa.' Emphatic screams. 'If Dua and I were together, would you ship us [imagine us in a relationship]?' More screams. But shipping just couldn't happen, Perry said regretfully. 'Not in this lifetime,' she added, because she was already spoken for. (She was then engaged to Orlando Bloom, with whom she had a daughter in 2020.) Extrapolating from that moment, it's safe to say that half the world had a crush on Dua Lipa.

Chapter 7

A NEW ERA

'A new era! Thank you for your patience. See you soon #DL2.' That post appeared on Lipa's Instagram account on 1 October 2019, just before she deleted every photo on the page, replacing them with a blank square. It could only mean that new music was imminent. On 1 November, it arrived. At least, the first single from the second album arrived: 'Don't Start Now', a discofied continuation of the 'New Rules' storyline. On the track, Dua is much further down the road to recovery after a break-up – so far down it, in fact, that she swats away an approach from the ex-boyfriend in question without a second thought. Look, she tells the chump, don't bother flattering me or trying to get me back. To emphasize the point, 'Don't Start Now's video begins with Lipa and her friends hustling the guy out of the club where he's followed her. Compounding his humiliation, once he's outside she shoves him to the ground with a 'Nnnnnrrrrggh!' The clip ends as Lipa stands over the recumbent body, probably giving him the talking-to of his life.

As a first taste of 'DL2' — the official title hadn't yet been revealed — it portended good things. A propulsive throwback to seventies disco, it not only revealed the musical leaning of 'DL2', it was also incredibly danceable and singable. Though she'd been anxious before releasing it — 'It [was] very different to what people have heard from me,' she told *Vanity Fair* later — it made it into many publications' Best Songs of 2019 lists, despite appearing just two months before the end of that year.

Illustrating its continuing impact, a year later it was No. 1 on *Variety*'s poll of 2020 songs (despite having come out in 2019) and was feted for the 'sense of liberation' it proffered in the first year of the pandemic. It was 'like a retrofitted "I Will Survive"', the magazine said, encapsulating the reason it was listened to throughout 2020. It hit No. 2 in both the US and the UK, and if it didn't reach No. 1, it still spent twenty-five weeks in the UK Top 10 and an entire year in the American Top 75. (Note that in the UK, it was kept off the No. 1 slot by 'Dance Monkey' by Australian singer Tones and I, which spent an unassailable eleven weeks at the top of the chart.)

The track got Lipa's second era off to a rousing start, and she might have allowed herself a brief sigh of relief. The success of *Dua Lipa* had piled pressure on her to exceed its sales with the second record — and the odds had been against it. When a new artist scores a smash straight out of the box, the probability of doing it again with the second album is discouragingly low. 'I wanted to get away from ... other people's expectations and opinions of what I should be doing because I felt like then I would try and recreate "New Rules",' she told *People* magazine. Then 'Don't Start Now' became a big track, followed by 'Physical' (UK No. 3) three months later and 'Break My Heart' (UK No. 6) in March 2020. Three substantial hits and *Future Nostalgia* wasn't even out yet.

Backtracking to late 2019, she followed 'Don't Start Now's release with two more big announcements. On 1 December, there was an Instagram post (she'd reinstated her social media by then) showing her in a bikini in front of tropical foliage. The caption said SWIPE FOR ALBUM TITLE. Swiping led to a close-up shot of her upper left arm, on which was tattooed 'Future Nostalgia'. Though the letters were small, cramped and slanted, they were decipherable – and that was the official announcement, right there.

She'd originally planned to title the album 'Glass House' after a line in the eventual title track, which would have worked on two levels: the song names modernist architect John Lautner, who designed an airy mid-century treehouse-style house in Studio City, Los Angeles, that she and Anwar Hadid bought as their California base in 2021; and 'glass house' was also a metaphor for the lack of privacy she'd experienced since becoming a well-known face.

As a title, however, *Future Nostalgia* had a more 'conceptual' feel, neatly summing up her thoughts as she began working on the album. In a press release that accompanied the 1 December album title announcement, she said she wanted to challenge herself 'to make music that felt like it could sit alongside some of my favourite classic pop songs, while still feeling fresh and uniquely mine'. But as 2020 unfolded, she had another reason to congratulate herself for the title: the term 'future nostalgia' evoked, in the words of critic Ken Tucker, 'a future of infinite possibilities while tapping into the sound and mood of some older music'. That precisely articulated the mood that had settled over the country as social distancing and isolation became the norm. For many, the only way to cope with the present was to hope for a brighter future while looking back at a seemingly golden, pre-Covid past. Several months later, she perceptively observed, 'Having [the album] out during the pandemic, it almost feels like immediately when we're out of it, the record will become nostalgic of this time period ... it will always be something that will remind me of this time period.'

When she first thought of the title – it came to her in October 2018, around the time she performed 'One Kiss' and her then new single 'Electricity' at the American Music Awards – Lipa couldn't have imagined how apt it would be. Nor could she have foreseen 'Don't Start Now' becoming a kind of social-distancing anthem. Its lyric was written purely as a 'get lost' to a former boyfriend, telling the guy not to go out or turn up anywhere near her. But a fan noticed that the words could equally apply to the newly introduced two-metres-apart rule and broadcast it in a tweet on 16 March 2020. It was headed 'How to avoid coronavirus' and quoted the lyric ('don't go out' etc.). It was swiftly liked 268,000 times and was noticed by Lipa, who tweeted back: 'I don't make the rules.'

The second major announcement, following that of the album title, came on 2 December. 'FUTURE NOSTALGIA TOUR — FIRST DROP OF THE WORLD TOUR — COME SEE ME IN A CITY NEAR YOU,' she tweeted. Underneath were twenty-four European dates, including eight in the UK, starting in April. On 21 February 2020, as the media was beginning to report daily updates on the spread of Covid — Britain had nine confirmed cases by that date — the Lipa team were still feeling confident enough to announce two further English shows, in Liverpool and Nottingham, on 29 and 30 May. Bearing in mind that it was a 'world' tour, further shows in the Americas and Australasia would have been in the planning stages and announced as soon as they were confirmed.

The new era, then, was coming along nicely. The album's second single, 'Physical', had made its appearance in January 2020, while the quirky title track had been released as a little bonus — not an official single — the month before. 'Future Nostalgia' had been the first song she wrote for the album, with A-list producer Jeff Bhasker (Drake, Beyoncé, Bruno Mars) and old confederate Clarence Coffee, usually known as simply Coffee. Bhasker got a namecheck in the first verse, in which Lipa credited 'Jeff' with creating the skittering bubblegum beat; likewise, Bhasker helped come up with the reference to John Lautner, also in the opening verse. Before they began writing, he and Lipa had a chat about architecture — one of her passions — and Lautner thus found his way into the song. As the very first track completed, it augured well for the songs that followed. The lyric presented her as a Lautner-esque game-changer, a 'female alpha' who dared men to keep up with her. Not your average pop star, in other words.

So, the album sessions began with 'female alpha' as her watchword, figuratively speaking. She later said she felt empowered by putting such terms into a lyric, receiving a confidence boost each time she sang them. She had evolved into a take-charge artist who trusted her own judgement, even if that meant, for instance, deciding not to use material she'd recorded with Nile Rodgers. The disco icon – 'icon' being the only word that fits – had spent time with Lipa at Abbey Road Studios in April 2019, and going by their subsequent social media posts, it was a productive day. Lipa wrote, 'Yesterday was truly one for the books. I was in the studio last night with the legend @nilerodgers and I was on the brink of tears ...' Rodgers's praise was joyously extravagant: 'I'm still flying high today after playing LIVE w/you at @abbeyroad. It was like Bowie [and] Madonna ... who trusted that my band would stomp on their music ... you are the real deal.'

Coming from the producer who had helped shape the *Let's Dance* and *Like a Virgin* albums, that was the highest possible praise. Yet when it came to assembling *Future Nostalgia*'s tracklisting, Lipa decided their collaboration didn't suit the record. She said she hoped that they could work together again, though, the prospect of which is tantalizing because Rodgers and Lipa are the best there is in their respective fields. The main point was that Lipa was now secure enough in her abilities to know when something did or didn't work.

The making of *Future Nostalgia* was both easier and more difficult than it was for *Dua Lipa*. On the upside, she was now a seasoned writer; working with longtime associates like Coffee, Sarah Hudson, Emily Warren and Koz, and new ones including Justin Tranter and Ali Tamposi, she penned sixty songs for *FN*, from which she picked the eleven that appear on the standard album. Some of the unused tracks turned up on subsequent *FN* repackagings, such as 'We're Good', which appeared on 2021's *Moonlight Edition*; it was notable for a piquant music video that starred a lobster who happened to be in a tank aboard the *Titanic*.

'I really feel I became a lot more confident during this whole album cycle,' she said via livestream on 26 March 2020, the day before the official release. Broadcasting from home, Lipa played snippets of each song and talked about how they were made. She contrasted the process to that of creating her debut, which had been 'such a learning curve. I was learning what was expected of me, what I had to do, how much I had to rehearse. At the same time, I was touring, travelling, doing promos, photo shoots ...'

Her newly hatched confidence was a reward for all the hard work she'd done. But she'd also lost something in the process: she began working on *Future Nostalgia* while promoting and touring *Dua Lipa*, resulting in a two-year stretch when there was almost no time to simply flop in a chair and let her mind go blank. Even for an artist with such an appetite for work that her record label uses her as an example to less energetic acts, that's a punishing workload. Yet she rarely admits to being tired, telling one interviewer that she's doing the job she always wanted to, so tiredness doesn't come into it.

On the 26 March livestream (Note that the sound failed after nineteen minutes, and she had to do a second livestream the following day), she described a system of working that boiled down to being constantly ready to write and record new material and also willing to give things a second chance. 'Cool', the third track on the album, is an example. In the early stages of collating ideas for *Future Nostalgia*, she and Joe Kentish, her Warner A&R, spent a good deal of time conferring about references and ideas, helped along by Lipa creating moodboards as visual representations of what she wanted.

Kentish had a song he thought she'd like and played it for her — and she hated it. The lyric didn't move her, and she was opposed to using other people's songs (it had been written by the production team TMS, Shakka Philip and Camille Purcell); please, she told Kentish, don't play this for me again. But he did, six months later — he'd stripped out the lyric and vocals and asked her to listen to the raw track. Without telling her what it was, he waited for her reaction. 'I love this! What is it?' she asked. It turned out that the raw track was perfect for her; she went into the studio with TMS and her friend Tove Lo, the Swedish alt-pop singer, and turned it into the synthy, playful 'Cool'.

'Physical', a co-write with Coffee, Sarah Hudson and pop hit-maker Jason Evigan, sprang from a desire to create something 'really eighties, really Flashdancey', as Lipa explained it. Her relationship with Coffee and Hudson is so close that whenever they write together, they end up dancing in the studio. 'Physical' is a piece of such ecstatic abandon they must have danced far into the night after the session.

Two 'Physical' videos were released. The first was a highly choreographed, visually stunning clip that took €500,000 and three days to make, and it won the Best Visual Effects category at the 2020 VMA ceremony. The second was a comic workout video in the style of Jane Fonda's genre-defining 1980s releases. Backed by a squad of dancers with names such as Tardy B and Upset (quite possibly modelled on rapper Cardi B and her partner Offset), 'exercise instructor' Lipa leads a keep-fit class in a gym as 'Physical' blasts through the room. Lipa appears to have a sixth sense about when to release music: the timeliness of putting out a mood-boosting disco album during a pandemic has been much discussed, but the workout clip was also a piece of inspired timing. It came out on 6 March 2020, a fortnight before the UK entered the first Covid lockdown, and as the population tried to adjust to self-isolating and #StayAtHome, what could be more welcome than a 'silly, whacky' (her words) five-minute exercise routine with Lipa as instructor? For those who wanted to take it a step further, her online shop just happened to be selling 'Physical' merchandise – the yellow leotard Lipa wore in the video is still available for a quite reasonable $39.95.

The track she singled out for special love on the livestream was 'Levitating', for its perfect blend of 'the future and the nostalgia element'. She saw it as directional – the first track recorded that truly caught the mood she wanted to create, it was written and recorded on the same day, as she and co-writers Coffee, Hudson and Koz ate doughnuts and danced across the studio. It was the one that assured her she was on the right path. The song was such a milestone that Lipa remembers the date it was written: 28 August 2018.

She was able to present it to Joe Kentish and her managers as the forerunner of the album's direction. When she started writing, Lipa had told them she wanted a record full of singles — 'only bangers', she said — and by the time it was finished, toward the end of 2019, that was what she'd made, while staying true to the 'future nostalgia' idea. Her management and label were proud of the progress she'd made since the halting, uncertain *Dua Lipa* sessions — she was now in the driver's seat while writing, manager Ed Millett revealed in March 2021. He gauged her progress as a writer by comparing her 'percentages' on *Future Nostalgia* to those on *Dua Lipa*. On the latter, she didn't co-write every track, but on the former, she was involved with every one.

By then, Millett was looking back at sixteen months of hit after hit: 'Don't Start Now', 'Physical', 'Break My Heart', 'Levitating' and 'Love Again'. The icing on the cake was that 2021 would finish with her third UK chart-topper, 'Cold Heart'. She played no part in its writing or music — it was an Elton John remix — but she received equal billing because her vocal was an integral part of its success.

Kentish and co-writer Koz agree that Lipa has the uncommon ability to know what she wants from the start of a project, which includes never settling for a sound or a beat that worked in the past. It has to be a new direction, which is why Koz loves working with her: she invariably '[puts] herself into her own lane', he told *Music Week*. Kentish was struck by her insistence on making *Future Nostalgia* with people she herself chose. When an artist is creating an LP with 'a really tight concept and sound', it's imperative to work with a small, focused group of collaborators. Dua's instinct for choosing the 'right' people – and she knew from the very start who she wanted – came from a sixth sense for the 'energies' they emanated. If the energy was right, they were in. Not coincidentally, she's become close friends with most of them.

The album's tracklisting, too, was exactingly sequenced. She decided it would open with the title track, with its scene-setting 'female alpha' reference, and close with 'Boys Will Be Boys', which called out toxic masculinity. Both songs were empowering and showed 'different sides of feminism', she said in the livestream.

And between the two? All bangers, just as she'd wanted.

Chapter 8

FUTURE NOSTALGIA

The album was originally due for release on 3 April, but Lipa had been agitating over whether to delay it because of the pandemic, as other big names, including Lady Gaga and Sam Smith, had. When lockdown began, she had been one week away from starting rehearsals for the Future Nostalgia tour. Both rehearsals and tour were now postponed, which threw a giant spanner in the works, as the album had been made with live performance in mind. As she'd worked in the studio, she'd even come up with a slogan: 'This is going to sound great at Glastonbury!' Suddenly, one of the album's main promotional channels – and almost its *raison d'être* – had been shut down. More immediately, she was scheduled to travel to New York to appear on *Saturday Night Live* on 28 March, a sought-after slot that was expected to get the US album campaign off to a rousing start. That would not now happen.

There were solid reasons to delay the album itself, perhaps until summer. For one, she was worried about seeming tone-deaf by putting out an upbeat pop LP in the middle of a developing health crisis; for another, the record might simply get overlooked in the flurry. There were also hopeful predictions that warmer weather might kill off the virus, so waiting for a few months could be beneficial. Instead, completely unexpectedly, she brought it forward to 27 March.

Not her choice — her hand was forced because the entire record had leaked, reportedly from a copy sent to a record store in advance. Things got even leakier when a widely read pop forum posted a link to the leak (it was quickly removed). With the stakes now changed — some fans were now calling her Dua Leaka — to delay would have been highly risky, no matter how laudable the reason. Her debut LP was nearly three years old, and its 'era', as fans call album promotional cycles, was over. It had produced eight singles and accordingly run dry as a source of fresh music. The eight had been followed by non-album singles that acted as placeholders, 'One Kiss' and 'Electricity', but if she didn't move on to the *Future Nostalgia* era quickly, momentum would be lost.

Technically, the era had already begun in November 2019, when 'Don't Start Now' had dropped. She felt a particular affinity with it, saying, 'I chose to put this song out first so I could close one chapter of my life and start another. Into a new era with a new sound.' The scorchingly dismissive lyrics had been generated not by her own love life but by an idea proposed by Norwegian singer-songwriter Caroline Ailin, who wrote it with Emily Warren and Ian Kirkpatrick. Ailin was worried about her ex-partner, who was missing her, and from that kernel a song grew.

Much later, in March 2022, Dua admitted that she hadn't felt as confident as she'd sounded. 'I was, like, "What am I even doing? Does anyone even want to hear this song?"' she admitted on the *At Your Service* podcast. In the same episode, she revealed that when her label heard the first few *Future Nostalgia* songs, they wondered if she knew what she was doing. 'The reaction was, "OK, disco ... interesting ..."' She informed them that disco was her inspiration and she was going to stick with it, especially because nobody else was doing it. She believed, even then, that she had an ear for sonically interesting directions, and she was proved right.

With *Future Nostalgia*'s first two singles, 'Don't Start Now' and 'Physical', reaching the Top 3 in the UK charts, the second era was shaping up to be more spectacular than the first, and it had been precision-tooled around a 3 April release. The expectation at Warner's was that the LP would definitely confirm her place on the pop-girl A-list—in other words, it *had* to be a hit. If it were anything less than a chart-topping behemoth, Lipa would be perceived as an artist who hadn't quite lived up to her promise.

Fans had been discussing it online for months, speculating about everything from the cover artwork, which was revealed in January 2020, to whether there would be features. When the tracklisting was unveiled, also in January, there was considerable disappointment that the standard edition contained zero features; every fan had a wishlist of potential Lipa collaborators, with Lady Gaga's name at the top of many a list.

A feature is a guest slot on someone else's song, usually arranged by the record label to broaden a track's appeal. Features aren't all they're cracked up to be; some artists cheapen their 'brand' by doing too many, some are barely audible on the finished song and often the featured artist isn't even in the studio at the same time as the main artist, so they never meet. Lipa is picky about features, as we'll see in Chapter 14. Another widely hoped-for *Future Nostalgia* collaboration was with American pop/R&B singer Normani, which actually already existed – it was a flavoursome pairing called 'If It Ain't Me', and it fully fit *Future Nostalgia*'s disco footprint. It leaked a few months before *FN*'s release, and when the tracklisting was revealed, many fans couldn't comprehend why it wasn't there. 'If It Ain't Me' has since attained almost mythical status because it eventually turned up on the *Moonlight Edition* of *FN*, in February 2021, but without Normani's vocal.

The sleeve art was widely praised for driving home – literally driving; Lipa was photographed at the wheel of a car – the 'future nostalgia' concept. Dressed in futuristic cut-out gloves and mismatched earrings and piloting what looked like a retro Cadillac, she could have been a Bond girl out for an evening's racing down the blacktop. As with all other elements of *Future Nostalgia*, the sleeve had been conceived as part of a glittery invitation to dance.

Much effort had gone into scheduling release dates for further singles, arranging media appearances and planning a second round of media promotion, to start several months after the album came out. If the record didn't materialize on 3 April, a very large applecart would be upset. A Warner's executive told *Music Week* that CDs were already in warehouses across America, making it impossible to change the release to an indeterminate time in the future because the CDs would be taking up space in the storerooms: 'It was leaking anyway, so we said, "We've got to roll."' Lipa herself felt that she and her team had invested so much emotional energy into the idea of an early spring release that to put it off for months would completely deflate them, making it hard to work up enthusiasm for promoting it when it did come out.

But with the leaked record now freely available online and Warner's prepared to release it rather than pause because of the pandemic, waiting until 3 April now looked like a bad strategy. It would have taken the wind out of the album's sails, in terms of both sales and the anticipation that had built in the run-up. A few fans were so loyal that they refused to listen to the leak – indeed, one fan site warned that asking for a link to the leaked material would result in a ban – but there was nothing for it but to get it out a week early, on 27 March. Lipa and her management authorized its release.

Their instincts were spot-on. *Future Nostalgia* entered the UK chart at No. 2, beaten by Australian boy band 5 Seconds of Summer's *CALM*, but a week later it was No. 1, making Lipa the first solo female artist to top the album chart in the new decade. In a more lasting sense, it would become known as the album that saw millions of housebound would-be partygoers through the pandemic. Joe Kentish said they learned a lesson from it: trust your gut.

A couple of months later, with the album safely out and basking in rave reviews everywhere (*NME*: five stars; *Independent*: five stars; *Entertainment Weekly*: A-; and on and on in the same adulatory vein), Lipa would breathe a sigh of relief. She'd smashed it – she wasn't going to be a one-hit-album wonder. In a giddy moment in June, she told the *Sun* that she was inspired by Madonna's career trajectory. The Queen of Pop had made album after landmark album during her twenties and thirties and 'peaked at forty or forty-five, and ... continues to kill it'. (Forty was her age when she released *Ray of Light*, seen as her renaissance; forty-five was the year of *American Life*, her brave but less-loved foray into socio-political commentary. Many would argue that Madonna's 'golden' era ended at forty-seven with *Confessions on a Dance Floor*, a joyous glitter ball of a record that was a clear influence on *Future Nostalgia*.)

Because of Madonna, Lipa added, women could now have decades-long careers that ended only when they wanted them to. For herself, she wanted to make music for as long as possible, and when she did retire it would be 'with a couple of dogs', and she would 'take up smoking again'. It's enjoyable to picture her in her garden in 2060, dogs scampering around, as she takes a satisfying drag on a cigarette. It seems that smoking has been hard for her to give up; some months after her comments to the *Sun*, she resumed the habit, quitting again in December 2021 while limbering up for the upcoming Future Nostalgia tour. She's

LEFT: Where it all began. In June 2013, Dua Lipa attends London Fashion Week in an early taste of celebrity life. Having moved to London alone at fifteen, all her hard work uploading videos of herself singing to YouTube and 'networking' at gigs was starting to pay off.

BELOW: Lipa performs on the main stage at Reading Festival in August 2018.

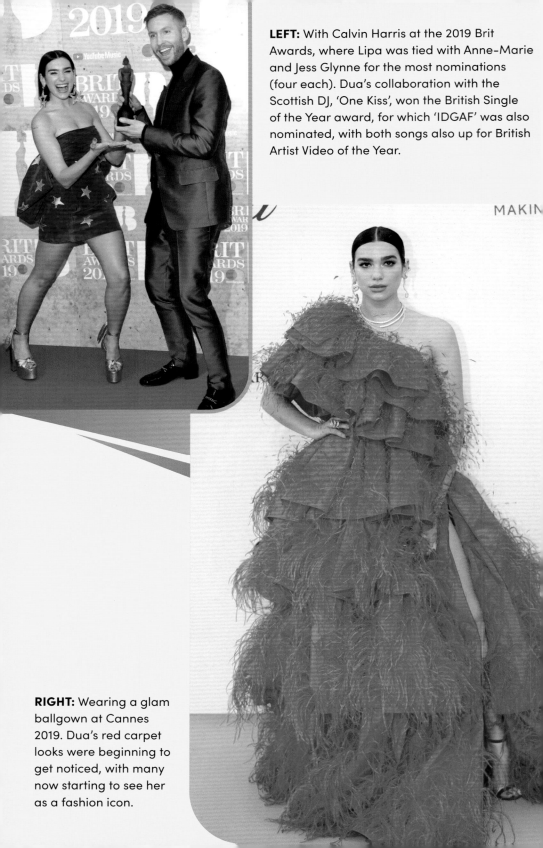

LEFT: With Calvin Harris at the 2019 Brit Awards, where Lipa was tied with Anne-Marie and Jess Glynne for the most nominations (four each). Dua's collaboration with the Scottish DJ, 'One Kiss', won the British Single of the Year award, for which 'IDGAF' was also nominated, with both songs also up for British Artist Video of the Year.

RIGHT: Wearing a glam ballgown at Cannes 2019. Dua's red carpet looks were beginning to get noticed, with many now starting to see her as a fashion icon.

ABOVE: 'I told them to believe in magic because it's real. And this is the closest I've come to it, so I wanted them to experience it first-hand.' The 2018 Brits was a perfect opportunity for Dua to share some of her success with her siblings, Rina and Gjin, as she pulled them up on stage with her to accept the award for British Breakthrough Act.

BELOW: The Lipa family caused something of a stir at the 2019 Brits, as host Jack Whitehall picked Lipa's dad Dugi out of the crowd. 'Do you know how much of a dad-crush I have? Your dad is the coolest dad,' Whitehall enthused. 'This is really getting out of hand,' Dua riposted as Whitehall went on to call her dad a 'silver fox'.

ABOVE LEFT: For the most part, Lipa has been able to avoid the rumour mill when it comes to her dating life. She dated brother of model superstars Gigi and Bella Hadid, Anwar, for two years until the end of 2021, with the pair calling off their romance as their careers frequently kept them apart.

ABOVE RIGHT: Still, with Lipa now embarking on her longest single period between relationships, media and fan speculation is never quiet for long. Here she is with rapper Jack Harlow in December 2022, his song 'Dua Lipa' leaving little doubt as to his feelings for the singer.

BELOW: Lipa with her songwriting dream team, Sarah Hudson and Clarence Coffee, in 2022. Together, the team have written some of Lipa's biggest hits, including 'Levitating' and 'Physical'.

ABOVE LEFT: Posing with her awards for British Album of the Year and Best Female Solo Artist, coming out as the artist with the most awards at the 2021 Brits.

ABOVE RIGHT: The awards for *Future Nostalgia* continued to pour in: here she is having won a Grammy for Best Pop Vocal Album, joining a prestigious list of previous winners and achieving one of the most renowned awards in the music industry.

LEFT: Having been ruthlessly mocked for her dance moves at previous award shows and gigs ('Go girl, give us nothing!'), at the 2021 Brit Awards Lipa grasped control of the narrative, showing off her new dancing prowess, the result of many hours' training.

RIGHT: With Megan Thee Stallion at the 2022 Grammy Awards, presenting the gong for Best New Artist. The pair recreated a 1998 skit between Mariah Carey and Whitney Houston, with Donatella Versace joining them on stage to amend their matching outfits.

BELOW LEFT: Achieving another feat beyond her wildest dreams. Dua and Elton John are now good friends, with Lipa performing as a support act at a number of the iconic rockstar's Farewell Yellow Brick Road gigs. Here, the pair are photographed at his 2021 Oscars party for the AIDS Foundation.

BELOW RIGHT: In September 2021, Dua was invited to walk the Versace catwalk at Milan Fashion Week. She was a natural model, adding some cheeky flair as she stuck out her tongue at the audience. It's fair to say she's come a long way since leaving her original agents when they told her she needed to drop 'a lot of weight' to make it.

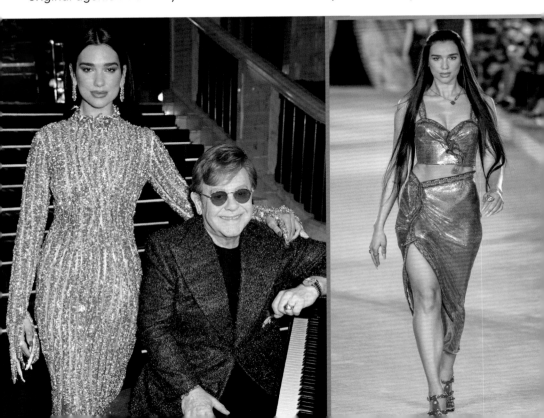

LEFT: At Sydney's annual Gay and Lesbian Mardi Gras parade in 2020. Lipa has made a name for herself supporting the LGBTQ+ community and throwing her weight behind political campaigns, even dedicating one of her many Brit awards to nurse Dame Elizabeth Anionwu and calling for higher wages for NHS workers.

RIGHT: Here, Dua performs with the Foo Fighters' Dave Grohl, Grace Carter and Ben Johnston of Biffy Clyro for Children in Need and Comic Relief's Big Night In in April 2020. As coronavirus impacted lives across the world, music became a balm for many, with Dua a leading figure in making Zoom work for the entertainment industry.

Dugi and Dua share the stage in Kosovo in 2016. As Dua's superstardom has risen, the pair have used their influence to set up the Sunny Hill Festival. The annual festival attracts some huge names, including Miley Cyrus, Calvin Harris and Stormzy.

The Future Nostalgia tour was one of the most hotly anticipated post-lockdown events, with Lipa putting on an enormous, throw-everything-at-it show for fans who had waited two years to see her perform again. With 'arenas full of fans going nuts', it can only be imagined what the superstar will do next.

stuck to it, she proudly announced on *At Your Service* in May 2022, with the help of a habit tracker app.

But just before *Future Nostalgia*'s early release, nobody could have predicted just how stratospherically her star would ascend. Expectations for the album and the tour that would promote it were high, but forecasting a pop artist's future is generally a hopeless game. Add the fact that this was the historically 'difficult' second album (the jokey rock-journalism term for the record that follows a very successful debut). Too many variables need to coalesce if the artist hopes to achieve large-scale, commotion-causing success. It's not enough to be talented, or to have the sort of drive that makes Mark Zuckerberg look like a slacker, or to be willing, as Ed Sheeran reportedly is, to closely monitor his worldwide chart positions and phone far-flung label reps if one of his songs has slipped a notch in their national chart. On that subject, while Lipa knows her sales statistics, she doesn't use them as a metric of success, perhaps because getting caught up in chart positions would detract from enjoying life.

It's not even enough to have brilliant tunes. Here it should be noted that during their 1970s superstar period, ABBA would release singles and have no idea whether they would be successful. 'SOS', 'Mamma Mia', 'Knowing Me, Knowing You' – they simply didn't know whether the record-buying public would like them. As Agnetha Fältskog revealed years later, the only exception was 'Dancing Queen', which was so undeniable that 'we all knew it would be massive'. And if ABBA couldn't judge which songs would be hits, who could?

Lipa knows the feeling. 'I can never [predict] what song is the one that people are going to react with best,' she told American chat-show host Stephen Colbert in 2022 – but occasionally she'll get a hunch. 'I had such a powerful feeling, being in the studio after writing "Levitating". We all felt so energized and so excited afterward.' Not only did the song dictate the overall sound of *Future Nostalgia* – 'it was the one where I felt, "OK, this is what *Future Nostalgia* is"' – but it became the most streamed track in the United States in 2021.

All these factors – talent, drive, ambition, great tunes – need to be present, and at just the right moment, which is where luck plays a part. Dua had the lot. Luck played such a big role in her early career that you can only guess at how things would have gone if she'd started several years earlier than she did. What if she had turned up before the UK music industry had decided that what it needed was 'a big pop girl'? Would she have been overlooked because it was the wrong time? 'Right place, wrong time' has been the undoing of many a hopeful's chances.

To go back to that earlier period for a moment: it should be understood that Dua, having long wanted to sing professionally, began trying to make it happen just as the UK music business realized it had no one who fit the 'big pop girl' (an industry term) brief. As we have seen, Warner Bros., in particular, was hunting for one. Britain hadn't produced a major female pop star in recent years. There was Adele, but she was a sophisticated balladeer; Jessie J had the pipes, but her larger-than-life personality wasn't for everyone; Jess Glynne had the songs but perhaps lacked charisma; and Rita Ora was ebullient and talented but not truly exceptional. The former members of Girls Aloud, meanwhile, had been brilliant as a band but didn't shine as solo performers.

Phil Christie, head of Warner's from 2016 to 2021, told *Music Business Worldwide* in 2017: 'As a modern major label you have to be operating with the broadest possible range. There were some areas we needed to compete in more strongly, and one was pop. Dua embodies that.' She was, he added, credible and talented – exactly what they were looking for in terms of a 'singular artist proposition' – industry-speak for 'solo artist'.

She had the voice, the determination and the self-awareness. She was also blessed with something that set her apart from many young singers: along with her self-awareness was articulacy and intellectual curiosity. She is assuredly the only pop singer who has ever mentioned John Lautner in a song (even the *Guardian* considered it 'too arcane a reference for a pop song', but surely that was part of its appeal). During her downtime on tour, she visits galleries and posts suggestions on her weekly newsletter, Service95.

A snippet from the Service95 issue dated 16 June 2022 says something about her erudition: 'I've tried (and I think succeeded!) to get my requisite dose of culture with a few museums and galleries I would highly recommend if you make your way to any of these incredible European cities.' The list that followed was headed by the Pinakothek der Moderne in Munich. Her suggestions convey her cultural literacy and the hope that everyone will share her delight.

A word here about Service95, a project she's colossally proud of and which was a long time in the making. It owes its existence to her habit of making lists, a lifelong compulsion. Some are strictly for self-betterment, such as a list of 100 books she wants to read before she dies (she has bought them all and is working through them, but new ones keep being added. Of the original hundred, her favourite was *The Unbearable Lightness of Being*). Other lists are compiled with the idea of sharing with others. Whenever Lipa travels, she writes notes on the best places to eat, stay, lounge around and view art and is so thorough that she's become pretty well an expert. Her family and friends now turn to her for advice on their own travels — even if they're only spending one night away from home, they consult Lipa about what to do when they get there.

It was obvious that this could become something to offer to people outside her social circle. Announcing it in November 2021, she set out Service95's sprawling remit: it would include the aforementioned recommendations, but also stories told from under-represented perspectives, articles written by activists and thinkers, newsy pieces about world issues ... it was a lot to take in, and boggling to think that Lipa, already impossibly busy, was proposing to shoulder yet another responsibility. The clue, however, is in the name. It's called 'service', because of her belief that her life's work is to 'be of service' to others — an extraordinarily generous philosophy not just for a pop star but for anyone, especially someone under thirty. (As for '95', it's her birth year.)

The breadth of her knowledge can be a surprise to those

who've enjoyed her music but who don't know much about her as a person. Anyone expecting a tame, malleable starlet will be wrong-footed; she's passionate about righting wrongs and fights injustice with a fire rarely seen in the pop industry. Service95 is billed as 'a style, culture and society concierge service', but it is far brainier than the slightly giddy gazette you might expect from that description.

Her convictions are strong, and they need to be. The internet swarms with racists, nationalists and misogynists who are hiding in plain sight, happy to share their opinions of her. Consider the racially charged question that appeared on the Quora website in 2022: 'Is Dua Lipa considered white in the UK?' It's pleasing to report that almost every reply said her race had no bearing on either her music or their enjoyment of it. Consider also a reader's comment under a recent newspaper article. The story itself was an innocent puff piece about the progress of the third album, but one reader replied, 'Go back to Albania.' Happily, the comment was resoundingly downvoted by other readers, one of whom informed the original poster: 'She was born in London, moron.'

Lipa will talk about politics if asked during an interview. She's pro-Black Lives Matter, pro-LGBTQ rights and pro-Labour. Regarding the last, she urged her fans to vote Labour in the 2019 general election. On 2 December 2019 she released an impassioned Instagram post addressed to her then 36 million followers: 'This is the most important election in a generation and YOUR vote counts ... See you at the ballot box 12th December! #VoteLabour.'

Cynics can ask whether any material difference is made by a pop star urging people to vote, but the fact is that it does help. A few weeks earlier, Stormzy had urged fans to register to vote – and 150,000 people under the age of twenty-five did. There are no figures to show whether Lipa's plea to vote Labour was heeded by her fans, but it's hard to believe she didn't have an effect.

Since childhood, Lipa has taken a stand on issues, urged on by her parents. From conversations that roved from their previous lives in Kosovo to their new lives in England, Dua gradually understood 'the politics of war, why so many children are displaced', as she told *Vanity Fair*. Curiosity drove her to read up on the subject, and the more she discovered, the stronger her feeling that she should represent others – something that impels her to this day. When Alabama banned abortion in 2019, she tweeted, 'FUCK THE PATRIARCHY I AM DONE WITH THIS BULLSHIT HANDMAIDS TALE SHIT WHAT THE FUCKING FUCK.' She meant every word. Three years later, after the US Supreme Court's decision to overturn *Roe* v *Wade*, the 1973 legislation that legalized abortion throughout the United States, she wrote, 'Woke up feeling miserable after yesterday's news about the overturn of *Roe* v *Wade*. It worries me deeply what consequences we will suffer due to this decision made by dinosaurs that won't even be around to live through this devastation.'

In July 2022, headlining the American super-festival Lollapalooza in Chicago, she attached a ringing endnote to her set. After recalling that her first 'Lolla' had been in 2016, when she'd played at two in the afternoon, she said, 'Stand up for women's rights, stand up against racial injustice, stand up for the LGBTQ community. Stand up for each other and I'm here to stand up for you in whatever way I can, I promise.' There was a time when few pop artists risked the career damage that could result if they expressed even the mildest political opinion, let alone a contentious one. Today, being pro-choice, pro-trans rights and anti-racism is hardly radical, but in some parts of the world her beliefs are still controversial. To which Lipa could reply that she's guided by a sense of what is right.

This is a side of her, though, that rarely crops up in her music. The only Lipa song, in fact, that directly addresses a political or societal issue is *Future Nostalgia*'s closer 'Boys Will Be Boys', which is the album's outlier in more ways than one.

The track, written by Lipa with Justin Tranter, Jason Evigan and Kennedi (who between them have worked with Justin Bieber, Lady Gaga and David Guetta), is compositionally different, incorporating strings and a choir; lyrically, it aims flat-out fury at the culture of entitled masculinity. Compared to the only other vaguely politicized song on the record — 'Future Nostalgia', with its boast that female alphas achieve their goals without male help — 'Boys Will Be Boys' is a direct statement about culturally instilled sexism. Boys will be boys and will stay 'boys' forever, according to the lyric, but girls have to grow up quickly and even then find themselves at the sharp end of male privilege and sexist expectations. One verse has a drippingly contemptuous reference to men riding to the rescue — and if any male takes that line seriously, the next adds that the singer is being sarcastic. She's also furious at having to 'mansplain' the sarcasm.

Her vocal is airy here, almost carefree, yet her intent is anything but. Notably, it was the one song on the album not much liked by some reviewers. Nothing to do with its content; it was just viewed as musically incongruous, this 'baroque' composition closing out an album full of bangers. In an otherwise rave review, the *Guardian* singled out the song as its sole weak spot. The reviewer was disappointed by the track's use of an 'earnest' children's choir — this was the Stagecoach Epsom Choir, with a membership comprising under-eighteens — because the subject matter would have been better served with a dash of 'Queen-like cheek', rather than pizzicato strings and kids chiming in.

In Lipa's defence, the choir are unobtrusive. This isn't one of those mawkish tunes where little voices heroically pipe along; the Stagecoach kids are subtle. Meanwhile, *Slant* magazine rather crushingly compared it to a power ballad — an 'enervating' finale to a record otherwise dedicated to escaping the now.

Until 'Boys Will Be Boys', Lipa's music had basked in almost unanimous praise. Most of the negative reaction to the song related to the music rather than the lyrical content, and Lipa will have taken note, perhaps deciding not to venture further down the avenue of children's choirs and string sections. Or she might decide not to be influenced by reviews and do what feels right.

Something we can almost certainly expect more of is social outspokenness. It's hard to imagine Lipa, who has recently talked of 'coming into my power' and no longer being afraid of discussing difficult things, being fulfilled by another album of relationship bangers. Guided by her conscience, her 'power' will see her addressing issues she hasn't previously touched on before in her music.

Chapter 9

A SENSE OF STYLE

Dua has loved music since the age of four. That, at any rate, was when she wrote her first song, which was in Albanian and addressed to her mother. The lyric went, roughly: 'When I grow up, can I borrow your dress? / When I grow up, can I borrow your shoes? / When I grow up, can I be as pretty as you?'

Bearing in mind her lifelong interest in fashion and style, it's fitting that her first self-written song was concerned with that subject, in the guise of a tune for Anesa. And by now, everyone knows the answer to the question, 'Can I be as pretty as you?' Lipa has the kind of streamlined beauty that makes fashion editors very happy, and as soon as she started making headway as an artist the fashion industry was interested.

British *Vogue*, the UK's most exalted fashion title, put her on the cover in November 2016, a decision that benefited Lipa and the magazine equally — her face was on every news-stand, while *Vogue* had landed the year's breakthrough act. The mutually beneficial relationship still thrives today, and Lipa has been on subsequent British *Vogue* covers, as well as on the covers of its sister editions in Turkey, Spain, Australia and — the biggie — America.

In that 2016 issue, the annual 'More Dash Than Cash' special, she modelled six outfits, all of which were wearable in real life — no Gaga-esque sirloin dresses here — and within the financial reach of fans who liked the look of that Adidas by Stella McCartney sweatshirt (a modest-for-McCartney £95) or the 3.1 Phillip Lim sweater-dress (£266). Inscrutably regarding the camera, Lipa was perfectly pitched between high fashion and London-girl cool, making the clothes, by extension, desirable. In the accompanying article, which approvingly noted her 'perfect pearly teeth', she professed an appreciation of the Marques'Almeida and Palace labels — again, aspirational but won't break the bank.

After *Vogue*, the floodgates opened, and today there's barely a style periodical that hasn't run a Dua Lipa cover story. She has such perfectly arranged, photogenic features that it's bewildering she wasn't more sought after during her brief go at modelling. The *X Factor* ad would have been a huge step in that direction — if, that is, Lipa had wanted to pursue modelling seriously. But her agency's weight-loss edict was too discomfiting. She was told that she'd get higher profile jobs, even catwalk jobs, if she were thinner, and she did, briefly, try to comply. It was so confidence-sapping that she withdrew from modelling entirely.

But she got the last word, twice over. First, the experience led directly to the creation of 'Blow Your Mind (Mwah)'. Lipa's pleasure as she wrote the song can be imagined: flipping a metaphorical two fingers at the agency and at those who laughed at her music-career aspirations, it says she's untameable and won't change for anyone else. She is who she is, and if anyone doesn't like it, there's the door.

Second, at Donatella Versace's request, she walked the Versace runway at Milan Fashion Week in September 2021. Catwalk work is tougher than people think, Versace told the media, and Dua had to do it in front of experienced models, making it that much harder. Lipa not only carried it off, she did it with some elan. Striding down the runway in a metallic pink two-piece, she was rigidly unsmiling in the time-tested way of the professional model — but as she reached the end of the catwalk and pivoted to go back, she winked and stuck out her tongue. This is just a laugh, don't take it seriously, she was signalling. 'We can safely say she killed it,' Versace told the *Wall Street Journal*. It would be pleasant to think that the wink was also aimed at her old agency: hey, look at me now!

A modelling postscript: in 2015, with debut single 'New Love' out and attracting tastemaker praise, Lipa signed to Next Models New York and found herself in demand for front covers and editorial. She's an adaptable cover star, able to turn her hand with equal ease to street fashion and the most haute of haute couture. If Lipa's innate elegance can't make an outfit look desirable, nothing can.

She proved the point during a weekend break in Amsterdam in October 2022, when she wore a Burberry outfit designed for the label's spring 2023 catwalk show. It was a black leather halter-cum-waistcoat and leather trousers, both oversized, though 'oversized' doesn't do justice to their volume, which was exaggerated by extra trouser material flapping around her legs. For chilly days there was an equally voluminous leather trenchcoat, as worn while Lipa explored the city with friends. The three pieces together were a classic 'challenging' fashion look — not one that many could have pulled off, and it wasn't Lipa's best style moment. (Even *Harper's Bazaar* called the ensemble 'unique'.) If *she* couldn't give the clothes zing and allure, it's safe to say no model could have. This is not to say that the outfit won't appeal to fans of striking design, but the general public will probably find the attraction hard to fathom.

But taking chances with style is her thing—'I love to experiment and play around,' she told Refinery29 in 2018 — and it extends to seeking out new designers in the cities where she tours. When in Amsterdam, say, she will try to wear clothes from an up-and-coming local, allying herself with them: fresh new designer as modelled by exceedingly stylish pop star. She also regards her penchant for edginess as a small gesture signalling progress toward a more equal world in which women can wear whatever they like without fear of criticism. Changing fashion norms in order to change the bigger picture is very much on her agenda.

Delightfully, she was also on the cover of the newly relaunched *Face* magazine in September 2019 wearing a knitted pink balaclava with long, upwardly thrusting rabbit ears. These 'custom mohair bunny ears', designed by Gareth Wrighton, made a pleasing change from the Dua-does-designer glossiness often found in cover stories. Inside, the main photo accompanying the interview was even better: an extreme close-up of her face, with a chameleon perched on her head. A live chameleon, clinging to her hair with scaly little feet. It looked more perturbed than Lipa, whose expression was tranquil. The photos were in the classic *Face* tradition of juxtaposing beauty with strangeness but also played up Lipa's sense of the absurd.

In the accompanying interview, she noted her inability to switch off – that if she's offered work that takes her fancy, she'll do it despite her schedule creaking under the weight of previous commitments. Attempting to slow down, she's tried meditation, but fell asleep. The thought arises that Lipa is the rare individual who requires little downtime because she's fulfilled by hard work.

She's 'psycho-organized', she told *Vogue* in 2022, slightly understating matters. Lipa is so organized that she knows when she'll be having a shower – it's in her schedule – and what she's having for breakfast every day. That tends to be eggs and fruit, consumed after a morning workout. Her 'exact diet' is available to scrutinize on various healthy-living websites; its preponderance of vegetables and fish is in line with the sort of nutrients she needs to fuel a physically demanding nightly show. When she has a day off, she might have a doughnut, but never on a work night because of the consequent 'food coma'.

As the hits stacked up and awards began to fill her mantelpiece, high-end designers vied for her patronage. She wore Armani and Valentino; Balenciaga designed the lacy neon-coloured outfits for the Future Nostalgia tour. For a *Time* magazine cover in March 2021, she was draped in an ankle-length pink Maison Valentino dress and wore Versace shoes – an outfit created to emphasize her height and poise. That issue saluted the publication's 2021 TIME100 Next list – a ones-to-watch feature that included authors, screenwriters, sports personalities and the Finnish Prime Minister.

The edition had six different covers, and Lipa being chosen for one affirmed her stature, though it was mildly puzzling that *Time* perceived her as an 'emerging' name when she had definitively emerged a good couple of years before. Each individual was the subject of a celebratory piece written by a well-known person; Lipa's was by Kylie Minogue, a great idol of hers. Kylie noted her instantly familiar voice, the 'clever' songwriting and her kindness and intelligence. Lipa was, she concluded, a 'pop behemoth'. This wasn't quite a handing-over of the baton – Minogue is as busy as she ever was and there's no replacing her – but the endorsement meant a good deal.

For designers, to dress Lipa was to score a major win: here was a woman who had hipster cachet and not only looked like a model but had actually been one. The fashion press has followed her tirelessly. *Vogue*'s archive alone brims with stories such as 'Dua Lipa's off-duty style is peak #Cabincore' (translated: a padded body warmer, shorts and baseball cap). *Vanity Fair*, meanwhile, got an entire article out of her 'Versace-inspired blonde hair transformation', which she underwent for the 2022 Grammy

Awards. The effort that went into lightening her natural shade was considerable, revealed her hairdresser, Chris Appleton, the man also responsible for turning Kim Kardashian and Ariana Grande into platinum blondes. By the time he and Lipa had finished a long day of bleaching, she looked – there's no other word for it – sensational. They decided not to lighten her roots because it was edgier; a cool girl would, of course, have dark roots (cf. Debbie Harry at her peak, who had not merely dark roots but entire brown sections amid the blonde). It would also dispense, at least for a while, with the need for retouching. In the event, no retouching at all was required; she reverted to her dark-haired self within weeks.

To complement the hair, Lipa wore a full-length black Versace gown to the awards, where she teamed up with Megan Thee Stallion to present the Best New Artist award to Olivia Rodrigo. As a bit of comic business, she and Megan found they were wearing the same dress, right down to the gold-link shoulder straps. After an instant's shock, Megan said testily, 'You stole my look!' Lipa huffed, 'I was told I had the exclusive. I'm going to have to have a talk with Donatella.' Enter Donatella Versace, declaring, 'Basta! Basta!' ('That's enough!') She dealt with the situation by tearing the long skirts off the dresses, leaving Dua and Megan in PVC leggings.

It was certainly a moment, and ... well ... it had been done before. In 1998, Whitney Houston and Mariah Carey, then two of the biggest stars in the world, had been mustered to present the trophy for Best Male Video at the MTV Video Music Awards, and both turned up in the same floor-length brown Vera Wang dress. Arguably, they had the edge on Megan and Dua on the funniness front. After a period of mutually icy staring, Carey said, 'Nice dress,' and Whitney rejoindered, 'You look pretty good too.' 'That's one of a kind, huh?' Carey asked. 'That's what they *told* me,' said Houston with perfect frosty timing. 'Fortunately, I come prepared,' Mariah announced, and ripped off the bottom half of her dress. What could Houston do but follow suit, and the ninety-second skit went down in awards-show history.

If Lipa and Megan borrowed, they borrowed from the best. But Lipa is better known for stylish individuality, as affirmed by the fashion industry's continued interest. In January 2023, it conferred a significant thumbs-up when US *Vogue* editor Anna Wintour appointed her co-chair – alongside Michaela Coel, Roger Federer, Penélope Cruz and Wintour herself – of fashion's biggest night, the Met Gala, a much photographed event staged annually at New York's Metropolitan Museum as a fundraiser for the museum's Costume Institute. The 2023 gala, themed Karl Lagerfeld: A Line of Beauty, takes place on 1 May.

Lipa is that rarity, a celebrity who's both credible and classy. And the answer to the question she posed as a four-year-old: yes, Dua, when you grow up you can be as pretty as your mother.

Chapter 10

FROM KOSOVO WITH LOVE

That untitled song she wrote for Anesa when she was four is Dua's first memory of writing music. The whole family was musical, 'so it was a natural gradient that I went into this as a career', she said on the podcast *Are We on Air?* Her parents' musical taste was her first influence; her nineties childhood was conducted to the sound of Moloko, Prince, Destiny's Child, Jamiroquai and – thanks to her father – Bob Dylan. That instilled a love of melody and bass, and later she fell for hip-hop.

She was in her teens and living in Kosovo then, and young Kosovars, she discovered, preferred hip-hop to almost any other genre. She has said that her first concert, when she was thirteen, was a Method Man/Redman double bill, and her second was 50 Cent. On the other hand, she's also declared that 50 Cent was the first, and history appears to support that version. On 17 December 2007, the American rapper, then promoting his third album, *Curtis*, became the first international musician to play Pristina. The concert promoter had originally tried to get Beyoncé, but she was unavailable at short notice; 50, however, was able to do it, and six weeks later he arrived, ready to dazzle.

Dua was one of 25,000 people who waited an hour in the open-air City Stadium as 50 made his way from hotel to show with his entourage of fourteen. In the great tradition of stars wanting to feel at home even when they're a long way from it, his rider stipulated that his hotel suite be painted red. (His support act, Kosovar rapper BimBimma, was nonplussed by the demand: 'How important is [red paint] to your mood? It's just unnecessary,' he said ten years after the event.) It was minus fifteen degrees, but in their excitement some people wore T-shirts and miniskirts. Twelve-year-old Dua had paid only €5 for her ticket, which came with a free SIM card handed out by IPKO, a newly launched local phone company that sponsored the show.

'I went fully prepared. Massive 50 Cent fan,' Dua said on *The Tonight Show* in 2019. Later, on the First We Feast *Hot Ones* podcast, she elaborated: 'It was freezing. Everybody was in their winter clothes. I'd learned all of 50's songs. I'd read the book, I'd watched the movie. I was super, super ready for the show. It lived up to all my expectations.' Her love of the music was, however, only part of the reason that 50 and Method Man were her first shows; the other is that they were virtually the only artists (along with Snoop Dogg later on, another gig she attended) willing to come to Kosovo. Since they'd made the effort to travel from America, half the young people in Pristina, Lipa included, felt it was only right to go to their shows. She would also have loved to have seen Nelly Furtado and P!nk, then at the apex of their careers, but few musicians were prepared to play in what was still regarded as a risky region.

To address exactly that issue, in 2018 Lipa and her father founded a multi-day music event in Kosovo. The Sunny Hill Festival, named after the Pristina district where Dugi and Anesa grew up, aims to attract top-flight international talent, who are supported by local acts. Dugi's experience of the UK music industry came into its own here. He was able to call on concert-promoting colossus Live Nation for advice about setting up the festival; two of its production managers came to Pristina to look at the site and provide guidance.

The inaugural line-up starred Lipa, superstar producer Martin Garrix and Albanian-American rapper Action Bronson as headliners, and a set by Dugi's former band Oda, who reunited for the occasion. In 2019, Miley Cyrus and Calvin Harris were the main-stage acts, and after a pandemic-forced break the event returned in August 2022, with Lipa and the collective might of rap and reggaeton's A-list: J Balvin, Skepta, AJ Tracey and Diplo. That year also saw the festival become a two-site event as it expanded into Tirana with a line-up headed by Stormzy.

Though the primary mission is to serve young Kosovars by presenting musicians they would never otherwise experience live, Sunny Hill has expanded into a charitable foundation committed to improving the lives of the most vulnerable people in the country. As of December 2022, the Sunny Hill Foundation has donated €100,000 to Kosovar cultural events and charities.

Dua is perhaps the only Kosovar with the clout to pull in names like Cyrus and Balvin. There, she's a hero — a woman who embodies the best of the country, acting as a counterpoint to the negative impressions sometimes associated with Kosovo. Dugi has ruefully spoken of this, telling the *Guardian* in 2018: 'When we first came to London you would tell people you were from Kosovo and nobody knew where it was. Then, later, everyone would say, "Oh, I'm so sorry." It was good that people had empathy but I don't want to be pitied. Then, with all the turmoil we had, parts of the problematic sector of our society migrated, and when you said you're from Kosovo, people thought about drug dealers or criminals. We want to show a very different image.'

Indeed, one of his main goals is to overturn the stereotypes that tarnish south-eastern Europe's image both inside and outside the region. In an interview broadcast in 2020 on the Romanian vlogger Pandutzu's *Backstage With* podcast, he discussed the mistrust that sometimes exists between Albanians, Romanians, Macedonians and Serbians. He didn't exclude himself. Recalling the time he dealt with a Romanian production company, he admitted that the Romanians were initially uncertain about working with a Kosovar, while his own kneejerk reaction was: 'Oh ... *Romanians.*' When the two parties got on with the job, they found common ground and parted friends.

The esteem in which Dua is held in Kosovo was made clear

when she played her first show there, in August 2016. She arrived at Pristina's airport and held a press conference — 'all in Kosovan', she said proudly afterward — then attended a reception to meet Kosovo's President and the mayor of Pristina. The gig was open-air, held in Germia Park, and 15,000 tickets had been sold. Roads had to be cordoned off. She was, she said before the show, terrified, but also happy to be coming back to show her Kosovar mates that her dreams of singing professionally had come true.

Six years later, in August 2022, she was invited to the Office of the President to receive the title of Honorary Ambassador. The invitation from Vjosa Osmani-Sadriu read in part: 'What you have done for the people of Kosovo, in raising awareness of the Republic of Kosovo, is unmatched and truly invaluable.' Lipa attended the ceremony with her parents, and the President brought her young twin daughters, one of whom is named Dua. She and her sister, Anda, presented flowers to Lipa; their excitement at meeting and hugging her was caught in a picture posted on the President's Instagram.

A beaming Lipa received a medal and a certificate that read: 'Titulli: Ambasador Nderi I Republikës Së Kosovës I Jepet Znj. [Ms] Dua Lipa.' The event was posted on both her Instagram and the President's. On Osmani's page, alongside a photo of her fastening the medal around Lipa's neck, the President wrote, 'Today I gave the title of Honorary Ambassador of the Republic of Kosovo [to Dua Lipa] because she continues to honour our country ... Today, because of Dua, there is no one who does not know Kosovo.' She lauded Lipa for her work on the Sunny Hill Festival, which had made Kosovo a world cultural centre, and for spreading the message about 'visa liberalization' for Kosovars. This latter point referred to visa-free travel to the European Union, which Kosovo has repeatedly requested since becoming an autonomous country in 2012. Kosovo is the only country in continental Europe (other than Russia and Belarus) that hasn't achieved EU liberalization, forcing Kosovars to apply for a permit to visit. Liberalization was the 'motto' of Sunny Hill's 2022 festival.

Lipa's work on behalf of Kosovo was recognized by the Washington DC-based think tank the Atlantic Council in its 2021 Distinguished Leadership Awards. In an honorees list that also included European Commission President Ursula von der Leyen and Albert Bourla, CEO of Pfizer, developers of one of the first Covid-19 vaccines, Lipa's name might have raised eyebrows, but her right to be there was absolute. Before she came to the stage, a screen scrolled through her achievements: advocate, philanthropist, supporter of charities and, yes, 'global superstar'. That day, however, she was there as 'a child of Kosovo, who was born and raised in the United Kingdom and is here today as a guest of the United States'.

Her six-minute speech was fluent, at times witty — 'journalists from highly respected publications speculate on what must be in the water to produce so many successful music artists' — and persuasive. The intention, in part, was to talk up the delights of Kosovo, a European country that most Europeans have never visited, and she did it as winningly as a tour guide. Lipa painted a picture of a 'very European' place with a lively café culture, a love of partying and a young population. Some 50 per cent are under the age of twenty-five, making Dua, then twenty-six, 'officially old in Kosovo'.

Appealing as such flashes of humour were, she might as well have dropped them from her address, because they failed to connect with the audience. It was likely that many there had never heard of Lipa or were simply surprised that a pop star should be an honoree. At any rate, her low-key witticisms were greeted with weak applause at best – even one that had been particularly gauged to raise a laugh. Addressing von der Leyen, Lipa said, 'I can only apologize for the sleepless nights my *other* country must have caused you during these long and painful Brexit negotiations.' There wasn't so much as a flicker in the audience until a few people politely clapped. Perhaps her British humour just didn't travel.

The other purpose of the speech was to announce a Sunny Hill initiative. Now one of the major music festivals in south-east Europe and the western Balkans, it was launching a foundation in Pristina. Lipa announced that a memorandum of understanding had been signed to create the Sunny Hill Arts and Innovation Centre, with construction to start in summer 2022. The centre aimed to work with young people who were interested in music performance and production; there would be workshops run by visiting musicians from around the world, Lipa promised. Kids who just wanted to build their confidence and learn a few skills would also be welcome.

Reminiscing about the first (or was it second?) concert she

went to, she acknowledged that the 2008 Method Man/Redman double-header was 'not quite age-appropriate' for a thirteen-year-old girl. But it wasn't as if she'd had any choice: 'Kosovo is just too small a market to be included on most world tours.' The Sunny Hill Festival has been filling that gap, bringing top-tier acts to an immensely appreciative audience. Without exception, she said, the visiting musicians have been 'blown away' by the atmosphere. Lipa knows from experience that the best performances happen when artist and audience have chemistry, and it always seems to occur at the festival.

Those at the Atlantic Council ceremony who had never heard her speak might have been surprised by her elegantly enunciated vowels. Pop stars are generally sold as everyday people from the neighbourhood, but if that's the case, Lipa's neighbourhood is a well-spoken one. *Rolling Stone* once characterized her pronunciation as 'a thick London accent', which in Britain would imply a strong working-class accent. The American publication, though, used 'thick London' to mean 'identifiably from the south of England'. Yet many Americans were amazed that she was English at all. Her singing is accentless, leading some in the US to assume that she must be from the States. It wasn't until they heard her speaking voice, at events like the Grammys, that they discovered the truth, provoking scores of 'What, she's *British*?' comments. For that exact reason, while recording 'Levitating' she inserted a couple of spoken lines so her accent would be plainly discernible: 'A lot of the time when I sing I guess people can't tell that I'm British,' she told *Song Exploder*.

She's not posh, but in the class-conscious pop industry, which frowns on artists who appear to come from privileged backgrounds, her accent stands out. It verges on received pronunciation – the supposedly 'standard' form of British speech, though RP now marks out the speaker as upper-crust. Lipa assuredly isn't that, but her accent is, with the exception of a sprinkling of glottal stops (dropping the 't' in the middle of words like 'little'). In fact, it's likely that her accent can be explained by two factors. She grew up in an area of north-west London – around the NW5 postcode – where many teenage girls adopt similarly upper-middle-class vowels; then there's the influence of Sylvia Young, where singing lessons emphasize the correct pronunciation of vowel sounds and the use of diphthongs – the sound made when pronouncing two vowels in the same syllable, such as 'cloud'.

Only a few singers who can justifiably be described as posh have managed to sneak into the charts in the past couple of decades. Florence Welch's family are so well-connected in the art world that Andy Warhol came to her parents' wedding; James Hillier Blount overcame the twin handicaps of a double-barrelled name and a captaincy in the Life Guards by renaming himself James Blunt and turning out to be handy with an introspective ballad. When social media arrived, he joined Twitter and swiftly made detractors change their minds about him, simply by being the funniest tweeter on the block. One of his most famous ripostes was his answer to the question, 'Why does James Blunt sing like his willy is being stood on?' He replied, 'Damn thing's always getting caught under my feet.'

Lipa, meanwhile, is just a girl from north-west London whose speech is deceptively refined but whose manner is resoundingly populist.

Chapter 11

A NOTICEABLY BETTER CLASS OF SONG

But how did Lipa progress from where she was in late 2019, when the Future Nostalgia tour was announced, to the top of pop's premier league? Though she was already known as a terrific singles artist in 2019, during the next three years she became something bigger and more enduring—not just a maker of reliably good tunes but, as the *Observer*'s Kitty Empire put it, an artist 'who is shaping up to be a pop star for the ages'. At this point, less than a decade into her career, it's premature to announce that she'll still be a pop eminence twenty years from now. But if any current star looks set to last the course, it's Dua.

Consider, for instance, that she was nominated for a 2023 Brit Award for Best Pop Act despite releasing just two singles — 'Sweetest Pie' and 'Potion' — in 2022. That reflects her stature and bodes well for the future. She announced it on 20 January, writing on Instagram and Twitter: 'Sending love from the Studio. I've been nominated for a Brit Award for Best Pop Act ~ voting is now open!! ... yippeeeeeeee.'

She's even had the ultimate accolade – a song named after her. It's a track on the second album by rapidly rising Louisville rapper Jack Harlow, *Come Home the Kids Miss You*. Judging by the lyric, he greatly admires Dua and, er, wants to get to know her. More graphically, he has a crush on her, and when she notices him he blushes, and ... you get the picture. Essentially, he wants to do 'more than just a feature' with her.

On 'Dua Lipa' Harlow isn't about to be fobbed off with a measly little feature on one of Dua's tracks, thanks all the same. There's some irony there as Harlow himself achieved major crossover success in 2021 thanks to a feature slot on Lil Nas X's 'Industry Baby', but he believes that merely adding a vocal to a Lipa song wouldn't win her heart. He wants to meet her and impress her in person. Before adding 'Dua Lipa' to his album, he sought her permission, playing her the song on FaceTime. She was nonplussed, Harlow admitted to the American podcast *The Breakfast Club*. 'She was like, "It's not my song. I suppose it's OK."' Harlow might have been hoping for more enthusiasm, but no matter. 'Dua Lipa' made it onto the album. It was criticized by some reviewers for not 'saying anything' about Lipa, but what more could have been said in what was basically a snappy little shout-out to a girl he fancied? And if reports are true, Harlow and Lipa began dating in late 2022, so 'Dua Lipa' worked.

Dua is equally exacting about recording material she hasn't had a hand in writing. She rarely does it, and the fact that she recorded 'New Rules', a track she didn't write, is explained by the fact that when songwriters Emily Warren, Caroline Ailin and Ian Kirkpatrick played it for her, she instantly warmed to its empowerment theme. There is some confusion about who the song was originally intended for. Pro songwriters often write on spec, generally with a particular artist in mind, and if the artist turns it down, the writer will then shop it around.

'New Rules's composers have said they always intended to present it to Lipa – but Kirkpatrick has also remarked that the original beneficiary was to have been a girl group, who declined because their label was unconvinced that it would make a splash. Apparently, they couldn't hear a 'substantial hook'. The song was shelved for a while, Kirkpatrick said, until it was sent to Lipa's management to see what she thought. Happily for all, she loved it. It was one of the best calls she ever made – at a stroke, she had the giant hit that made the difference between 'very successful' and 'next stop: superstardom'. Even now, it would be interesting to know how the girl group – said to be Little Mix – could have missed its potential.

But 'New Rules' was an exception for Lipa. Her usual policy was to turn down songs or feature requests by other writers if she hadn't been involved in their creation, and she stuck to it fairly rigidly. This attests to her integrity but means she's missed out on tunes that could have been smashes. Some material she was offered was so obviously destined to be huge that Ben Mawson was frustrated — it was a 'dilemma', he said, because when she didn't like a track, that was it, she wouldn't do it, even when her label advised that it would be a great fit for her.

Several features that she passed on became smashes for other female singers, including one that Mawson refused to name, which went on to be one of the biggest singles of that particular year. It made no difference; Lipa's code of conduct forbade her jumping onto a song just because it sounded like it might do well.

The explanation for Dua's dizzying ascent might be as simple as something noted by *Guardian* critic Alexis Petridis in his review of the 2022 Manchester show: 'What Dua Lipa has, and has in profusion, is a noticeably better class of song than any of her British pop peers.' He wasn't wrong about that. Her two studio albums are loaded with more earworms than many artists manage in an entire career — but that in itself doesn't produce a pop star for the ages.

Before we get to that, let's briefly run through the singles Lipa put out during her *Dua Lipa* era. It yielded 'Be the One', 'Blow Your Mind (Mwah)', 'Hotter than Hell', 'IDGAF' and 'New Rules', along with the less successful 'New Love', 'Last Dance' and 'Lost in Your Light'. That's an impressive tally for a first record, and each was a fantastic tune that has stayed fresh despite endless radio play and streaming. 'New Rules' was a particular corker; it became her first British No. 1 single, with *GQ* praising the 'contralto girl-anthem'.

In America, 'New Rules' peaked at No. 6, but it still sold 5 million copies there — an extraordinary achievement for a British singer. (By the way, as for applying the 'new rules' to her own real life, Lipa doesn't always manage it. 'They're not necessarily rules I've been able to stick by but rules that I feel like it's important to be able to tell yourself,' she said in an NPR radio interview.)

Thus, as *Dua Lipa*'s era closed and Future *Nostalgia*'s began, she had already climbed a fair way up the Proper Big Star ladder, and playing arenas on the tour she'd announced in December 2019 would be another rung upward. Then the world locked down, and Lipa's new record took on a life of its own.

The reaction to *Future Nostalgia*'s first singles was so positive that it seemed the 'difficult second album' wouldn't be quite so difficult after all. But the timing of its release, against the backdrop of coronavirus, had an effect that was impossible to have foreseen. First, there was an Instagram announcement from Lipa on 23 March, the day Boris Johnson announced strict measures aimed at combating coronavirus. In a lengthy livestream, she cried as she told viewers she had changed the release date from 3 April to 27 March. She wasn't sure she should be putting out a record at all, given 'the uncertainty of everything'. Would it seem frivolous, she wondered, at a time when 'lots of people are suffering'?

She was livestreaming from home, except that 'home' was an Airbnb, hastily rented because, two weeks earlier, she had got off a twenty-four-hour flight from Australia to find her flat flooded. Her upstairs neighbour had been renovating their place, causing water to trickle through her ceiling for the fortnight she'd been away. Her apartment now needed renovations of its own, and she'd moved into a 'random', as she put it, Airbnb with Anwar Hadid.

Before she'd even begun work on *Future Nostalgia*, she was warned by industry associates that the second album would be tough. The pressure of following a 6-million-selling debut would be considerable, she was told, and she should manage her expectations. In response, she 'shut all that out', gathering a group of writers and producers she considered friends and going into the studio until she had made 'something I was proud of'. The aim was to create music that would lift people's spirits and make them dance. Bearing in mind that the sessions started in January 2018, she couldn't have known how welcome such an album would be in March 2020.

With the release of *Future Nostalgia* now just four days away, she was emotional – so much work had gone into it, but it would be coming out at a point when talking about pop music, let alone listening to it, felt almost indecent. Weighing it up, though, Lipa had decided that the record could act as a corrective to the prevailing mood of anxiety. 'The thing we need most at the moment is music, and we need joy ... Make of it what you will. I hope it brings you some happiness and I hope it makes you smile.'

Lipa brightened when she reached the subject of her new single, 'Break My Heart', due for release two days later. 'I'm excited, because it's my forte, which is dance-crying' – her term for a style she'd made her own, fusing romantic despair and spectacularly catchy, anthemic melodies. Much of her strongest work, such as 'New Rules' and 'Hotter than Hell', uses the dance-crying template, but 'Break My Heart' is about heartbreak that hasn't even happened – pre-emptive heartbreak, perhaps. It was about her relationship with Hadid, whom she had been seeing since the previous summer after meeting him at a barbecue.

The song acknowledges her excitement and delight at being with him but broods about the possibility that it could all go pear-shaped. 'It's a celebration of vulnerability,' she said, and the lyrics certainly support that. She lays herself on the line, telling her beloved that all he had to do was say the word and she would be there. That kind of soul-baring can often be counterproductive, and Dua is aware of that, because in the chorus she wonders whether, having opened her heart to him, it will get broken. She and Hadid did split up in late 2021, apparently because their careers frequently kept them apart. They had been 'in crisis talks', claimed the *Sun*; 'We're trying to figure it out,' Lipa said, but it was to no avail. Did she observe her 'new rules' after they parted – refraining from phoning Hadid, refusing to be friends and so on?

Note that 'Break My Heart's writing credits include Michael Hutchence and Andrew Farriss of INXS, whose 1987 single, 'Need You Tonight', provided inspiration (its guitar riff is similar to a synth line that runs through 'Break My Heart').

Future Nostalgia duly came out on 27 March, entered the UK chart at No. 2 and reached the summit the following week. In the US, her biggest market after Britain, it got to an extremely respectable No. 3. But it was the unquantifiable events after its release that led to Lipa's elevation to Alpha Pop Star.

The reviews were near-unanimous raves, which always helps.

And they were no-holds-barred raves: the album was 'a pop behemoth', said the *Observer*; the *Guardian* deemed it 'outlandishly great' and Dua herself 'a pop visionary'; elsewhere, it was 'high-octane pop bliss', as far as *Entertainment Weekly* was concerned, and AllMusic summed up what the others were thinking: '*Future Nostalgia* could have just as well been titled *Future Classic*.' You can't buy coverage like that.

Significantly, there were no ballads on the record. The entire thirty-seven minutes bubbled over with dance-music energy — and alongside that, equally significantly, was the 'nostalgia' element. The songs intentionally referenced the past, with salutes to Donna Summer's 'I Feel Love' on the woozy track 'Hallucinate', to Olivia Newton-John's 'Physical' on Dua's identically titled disco rave-up, and to Lily Allen's 'Smile' on the deceptively sunny 'Good in Bed'.

Word of 'Good in Bed' made its way to Allen herself, who addressed the subject during an online chat with fans just after *Future Nostalgia* leaked. She revealed that her timeline was laden with messages drawing her attention to the fact that *FN* contained 'a song called [long pause as she tried to remember the title] "Good in Bed" that sounds like me'. But she'd also seen comments claiming that it was 'the worst song on the album, so ... thanks, guys'. Allen didn't say whether she'd heard it, but her bemused expression suggested it was all news to her.

'Good in Bed' and 'Smile' are distinct songs. They share certain characteristics, but you couldn't mistake one for the other. Lipa's tune, which she wrote with Michel 'Lindgren' Schulz, Denzel

Baptiste, David Biral, Taylor Upsahl and Melanie Fontana, does share a breeziness with 'Smile', and Dua's vocal and Allen's are similarly airy. Both tracks, too, are angry under their delicious buoyance. Lipa is bitterly taking stock of a relationship in which a blazing sex life is the only enjoyable aspect of a partnership that's failing in every other way. Meanwhile, Allen's song relates her pleasure at witnessing the downfall of a cheating boyfriend. In the video, she pays to have him beaten up, and when the boyfriend comes to meet her in a café, freshly bruised from the back-alley attack, she refuses to take him back. The song title comes from the smile that creeps across her face and becomes a laugh when he phones to apologize for his behaviour.

But 'Good in Bed' doesn't replicate 'Smile's melodic structure – the resemblance is all in its buoyant charm. Allen wasn't one of Lipa's formative musical influences, either. Though she would probably have approved of Allen's lyrical honesty and sharp intelligence, she was just eleven when 'Smile' came out in 2006 (its B-side, marvellously, was 'Cheryl Tweedy', after the Girls Aloud singer, but its bubbly arrangement contrasted with a sharply self-critical lyric about wishing she looked like Tweedy). At eleven, Dua was completely devoted to Nelly Furtado and P!nk, and few other singers got a look-in.

The lyric video accompanying 'Good in Bed' was another illustration of the 'nostalgia' part of *Future Nostalgia*. It began with a thumb pressing 'Play' on a 1970s cassette recorder, followed by the song blaring from its tiny speaker. Music playback devices don't get more retro than a boxy tape player with only six buttons: 'Play',

'Stop', 'Fast Forward', 'Rewind', 'Record' and 'Eject'. For a woman born in 1995, the tape recorder must have seemed as antique as a wind-up gramophone did to her parents' generation.

In essence, *Future Nostalgia* was pure dance-pop with a strong throwback vibe. In keeping with the aesthetic, it contained no collaborations with other singers, making it an exception to the twenty-first-century practice of drafting in big names in order to appeal to two fanbases at once.

Dua is no stranger to features, having done them with Calvin Harris, Megan Thee Stallion and many others, but the standard edition of *Future Nostalgia* is notably feature-free. It wasn't that she'd been averse to the idea — she'd considered collaborating but couldn't decide who would be best suited to the songs, and in the end released them as they were. However, a later version released in February 2021, *The Moonlight Edition*, was studded with features and collaborations she'd made earlier and 'kind of put aside for a second wind', she told the UK digital station Kiss. Among those included were 'Prisoner' with Miley Cyrus and a version of 'Levitating' that featured American MC DaBaby.

DaBaby's version far outpaced the original, non-collaborative version of 'Levitating' in popularity: compare the original's 4 million YouTube views with 675 million for DaBaby's remix. The huge difference is accounted for by a couple of factors. In the US, where the rapper was at the height of his popularity thanks to his recent No. 1 single 'Rockstar', his version was promoted by the record company as the official single and as such was all over American radio.

Then there was the simple fact that his contribution to 'Levitating' added even more sugar-coated fun to an already bubbly tune. His flow was an energetic counterpoint to Lipa's seventies bubblegum vocal, and in the accompanying video his impact was even greater. Making his appearance fifty-two seconds in, decked out in frankly challenging flowery Louis Vuitton shorts and sweater, he was swaggering but ebullient, self-aggrandizing but smiling. All told, he stole the show. Lipa anchored the clip by being reliably effervescent, but DaBaby added pizzazz.

During one of his own shows in Miami in July 2021, the rapper, whose real name is Jonathan Kirk, made homophobic remarks that resulted in many radio stations dropping his version of 'Levitating' from playlists. Though he claimed that his comments were just concert banter, the reaction from all but hardcore fans was overwhelmingly negative. Lipa was 'horrified', writing on Instagram: 'I really don't recognize this as the person I worked with.' Kirk quickly apologized, saying he would learn from the experience, but within a few days deleted the apology without explanation. Subsequently, he was dropped from the line-ups of a number of festivals, and brands he represented cut their ties with him. They included boohooMAN, which had released a clothing range with him only a month before. He still has a considerable social-media presence, including 21 million followers on Instagram and 4.5 million on Twitter. Needless to say, Dua remains solidly committed to the campaign for LGBT+ rights.

Future Nostalgia's title suggested that we would one day look back on this era with the same yearning we now feel for past decades. While we waited for that 'one day' to arrive, this was the perfect album for anxious times. That's not what Dua had planned, but that's what it became. All she'd intended, she said, was to make a record that reminded her of the music her parents had played when she was a kid: not just danceable acts like Moloko, Jamiroquai and Prince but David Bowie, Radiohead and (a particular favourite of her dad's) Sting. 'I have such fond memories of that music,' she said on the American morning talk show *Live with Kelly and Ryan*. 'I wanted to build on those memories and that feeling and that emotion and create something that felt modern and new at the same time.'

The record turned out to be a soundtrack to lockdown. Other well-known people had innovative ideas for coping with quarantining, too: Sophie Ellis-Bextor had her Kitchen Disco; Tim Burgess his Tim's Twitter Listening Party; Joe Wicks his PE with Joe workout videos. To that list can be added *Future Nostalgia*. Though it was finished well before the pandemic took hold, with three singles already released, it was every bit as comforting and diverting as Ellis-Bextor's Friday-night performances in her home and Burgess's simple device of playing a famous album online and having the musicians who made it tweet about each track as it played.

That first single, 'Don't Start Now', was a fantastic taste of the LP. Not only was it motivational, it was also wildly catchy because, said *Stereogum*, it was 'straight-up disco, baby, dirty bassline and sumptuous strings and all'. It was a worldwide hit, selling 4 million copies in the United States alone, and settled the question of whether the brilliant songs on the debut album had been merely beginner's luck. Answer: no.

The title track, released as a bit of a lark in December 2019 because it showed her and producer Jeff Bhasker 'not taking ourselves too seriously', was worth hearing in its own right because it featured her rapping. Her rap style was a silky torrent that wouldn't give Megan Thee Stallion sleepless nights but was engaging nonetheless. In the verse where she identified herself as a female alpha, it was the first time Lipa had acknowledged her growing power and influence.

Once *Future Nostalgia* was actually out, the great singles kept coming: 'Hallucinate', 'Levitating', 'Love Again', 'Fever' (from the album's French edition) and 'We're Good' (a bonus track that didn't make it onto the original album but was good enough for the 2021 *Moonlight Edition*). Dropping a steady stream of tracks didn't just keep the album alive in the chart, it kept Lipa in the public consciousness. She should have spent the spring of 2020 on tour, but when that became impossible the next best thing was getting a slew of new songs out. Wherever you were in 2020, you were never far from a TV or a phone playing one of her tunes. In an interview Lipa remarked, almost with embarrassment, that even she couldn't get away from herself: she'd get into her car, turn on the radio and there was her voice. She was almost as 'present' as she would have been had her tour taken place as scheduled, from April to June 2020.

And she kept working throughout 2020, doing promo (interviews and photo shoots to promote the album) and occasional performances from home. One of those was a *Tiny Desk (Home)* concert in December – mentioned here because the selling point of the US-based series is stripped-down minimalism in the vein of the old *MTV Unplugged* shows. Musicians play with no embellishment, often acoustically, showing a different side to their artistry. Minimalism isn't a word associated with a Lipa live performance. When she's on a stage, it's all about maximalism: choreography, costumes, elaborate stage sets. Did anyone even know how she sounded in a small room with all the stagey bits removed? This was her chance to show what she could do.

Which she did. Backed by four singers, a guitarist and a bassist, Lipa turned in sixteen minutes of pure voice-centred delight. Socially distanced in a softly lit living room (she said they were in 'our London home', in which case the seven of them lived in a trendily pared-down, loft-style apartment), the group turned down the volume and allowed her vocal to dominate. What's not always evident from Dua's records is how well she sings – moreover, when she's in the middle of a high-volume stage show, it's easy to overlook her richness and control. The *Tiny Desk* set put those qualities front and centre.

Of the four songs played ('Levitating', 'Pretty Please', 'Love Again' and 'Don't Start Now'), 'Levitating' was particularly moving. Yes, moving – this frothy love song acquired gravitas when the tempo was slowed a bit and the lyrics sung caressingly. Compare it to the way she performed the same song on the Future Nostalgia tour. On the big arena stages, 'Levitating' was a show highlight, sung while standing on a metal 'levitator' that glided serenely across the arena, 20ft above the crowd. Lipa delivered the song briskly, as would anyone who had to concentrate on both singing and holding the rail of their levitator. When it finally landed on the stage, she was joined by a dozen dancers and the show whirled on, loudly and fabulously. Whatever vocal clarity is lost during her arena sets is worth the sacrifice, when the trade-off is a show of such glittering pleasures.

Lipa's shows now are all about the spectacle, and they provide plenty of bang for your concert buck. Her productions have come a very long way from two shows reviewed by the *Guardian* in 2016 and 2017. She was playing small venues and of necessity didn't have much of a 'show' — in January 2016, she was backed by two guitarist-keyboardists and a drummer, and that was it. Even if she'd wanted to bring along a dancer or two, there was no room on the stage, which was upstairs in the Hope & Ruin pub in Brighton. Without the distraction of costumes and special effects, her voice dominated proceedings, and it was a voice that punters remembered afterward. The *Guardian* said as much in its review: 'Mainly, though, she can sing. Debut single "New Love", which got her voted into the BBC Sound of 2016 longlist, showcases a smoke-darkened voice older and more disillusioned than her years.'

Fifteen months later, headlining the 2,000-capacity Shepherd's Bush Empire in London, she was still all about the voice. 'She uses her big voice like the nuclear deterrent — even when she delicately glides through the acoustic number "Thinking 'Bout You", we're fully aware of the torrent she's damming up,' the *Guardian* said.

At these early moments in her live-performance career, Lipa let the music do the talking, which is to say that she didn't exude much in the way of personality. That would change, but for now, audience interaction was limited: she said hello, introduced the songs and thanked punters at the end. The *Guardian* saw this as something that needed working on: 'Lipa just comes across as having nothing much to say. Her set opens with a murmured "Brighton, what're you saying?" and ends with "This is the last song." During the forty minutes in between, she gauchely fails to acknowledge that there's a gaggle of fans here who like her enough to have learned all the words to "New Love" and current single "Be the One".'

With hindsight, that was immaterial. The 100 or so people at that pub, who had probably discovered her before she was voted onto the Sound of 2016 list, weren't pernickety about whether or not she chatted during the set. For many, it was enough just to be in a small room with a rising star – being able to say they'd seen her in a pub would make a good story if she became famous. And did anyone have the right to expect more of her at such an embryonic moment?

And it could work both ways. At a show in Paris around the same time, she made a real effort to engage the audience, who had been watching impassively. There was a gap between the stage and the front row, and she invited them – commanded them – to move closer. Not a soul budged. Discouraged, she did the rest of the set in front of this crowd, taking their coolness as a sign that they didn't like her.

Getting up on stage could be daunting, Lipa explained to *Attitude* magazine in September 2017: 'You kind of don't know what to do when there's so many people just staring at you.' She'd only done her first full concert in January 2016, at the Eurosonic Festival in the Netherlands – just four days before the Brighton show reviewed by the *Guardian*. Like many up-and-coming pop artists, she'd prioritized writing and recording over going on the road; gigs could wait until there was a bundle of songs to play live. Only when a new artist takes their first steps into live performance do they discover how tough it is, and it's not a craft that can be taught in a studio. Of current pop titans, Ed Sheeran is virtually the only exception to that rule; he busked and played pubs for years before setting foot in a recording studio.

At Shepherd's Bush the following year, she was still something of a cipher on stage, releasing her feelings in the songs but saying little during the gaps between them. Around that time, Lipa told an interviewer that she was learning to be more communicative, but it was obvious that she had some way to go. 'The deciding factor ... will be whether the vulnerability she pours into her lyrics is ever allowed to impinge on the functional, slightly generic self she presents on stage,' the *Guardian* reviewer wrote. 'With everything to play for, though, don't bet against her.'

Only a fool would have bet against her. Lipa simply had so much going for her that it was impossible to write her off. She had only recently been shortlisted for the 2017 Brits Critics' Choice Award (the winner was Rag'n'Bone Man, but the exposure brought her to the notice of many who hadn't encountered her before). Her debut album was about to be released. She'd already had four Top 30 singles in the UK. All this stuff added up—she was one of Warner Bros. Records' priority acts for 2017, and each small triumph—the Critics' Choice list, selling out 2,000-seaters—was another step toward the first tier of pop.

She was so sure a bet that even an underperforming collaboration with R&B crooner Miguel called 'Lost in Your Light', which emerged a week after the Shepherd's Bush date, didn't slow her down. (It peaked at No. 86 in the UK and made no impression at all on Miguel's home turf, the USA — a rare flop for both.) It made no odds because Warner's had the next single lined up and were banking on it being a career game-changer. It was 'New Rules', scheduled for 7 July, and the label's faith was justified.

It was her first British No. 1, the first of her songs to be adopted as an empowerment anthem by Gen Z and her first single to make it to many end-of-year lists. *Time* magazine, naming it the best song of 2017, viewed it as something even greater than 'an escapist fantasy of girl power'. With the world still absorbing the shock of Donald Trump's inauguration the previous January, *Time* commented, 'No year has needed new rules as desperately as 2017 did ... it's an anthem for self-care in a moment when so many of us felt unmoored.' The *Guardian* made an equally pertinent point: 'This is why it's impossible to be a music snob in 2017: "disposable" pop is now actually this good.'

Back to 2020 and *Future Nostalgia*. There was no respite from promotional duties throughout that year, and on top of the usual stresses of a major album launch was the fact that she was doing it all from home. That brought the pressure of maintaining a suitably glamorous appearance for the many TV interviews she carried out. Having to manage without a hairdresser or make-up artist is the quintessential first-world problem, but getting beautified before facing the public *is* part of a pop star's job – the sort of thing that can't be abandoned without incurring social-media jibes. Here it helped that she was in her mid-twenties, naturally attractive and had make-up skills she'd learned while modelling.

Lipa also had to learn to make her own green screen – the special-effects backdrop used by video editors to virtually show different backgrounds. Just two weeks into lockdown, she created one for Jimmy Fallon's *Tonight Show* when she performed 'Break My Heart', her just-released single. Instead of the brick interior wall of the flat where she was quarantining, viewers saw Lipa's backing band, dancers and city streets, all conjured up via her laptop. Fallon owed her a debt of gratitude for that: she was the first lockdown guest who made a green screen, and once she'd done it others followed suit.

The importance of that is hard to overstate. A show like Fallon's is given extra zazz by its musical guests, but if they're not there with him, playing live in Studio 6B at 30 Rockefeller Plaza, they need to be extra-captivating in their remote location. Playing in front of a bare wall, even of necessity, will only emphasize the unreality of performing during the pandemic. Lipa's green screen turned what would have been a bare-bones rendition of 'Break My Heart' into a performance. Two years later, when she joined him in real life in the New York studio, he hadn't forgotten. 'I can't thank you enough for that,' he said, as Lipa graciously waved it off, saying that she'd also learned something in the process. (To see a more elaborate use of a green screen, check the video for 'One Kiss' and its parade of playful, quick-changing backdrops. One moment she's singing in front of the sun rising out of the sea, the next she's in a desert and a bit later a giant yellow flower engulfs her.)

Throughout *Future Nostalgia*'s promotional period, she was patient and charming, even during encounters like an appearance on an American chat show where she was asked what the British dish 'bubbles and squeak' was. Politely overlooking the misnaming — it's 'bubble', singular — she explained that it was a mishmash of whatever was in the fridge. 'I might have that wrong,' she added, 'which makes me a terrible British person.' But she was also amusing and self-deprecating, which makes her a great British person. (NB purists would argue that true bubble and squeak consists of leftover potatoes and cabbage, fried in butter, but the modern cook is more apt to throw in other ingredients, such as more veg, bacon or a poached egg, making Lipa's an acceptable version.)

In October, she announced that the tour dates, which had been pushed back to January 2021, would now take place in September 2021. To assuage fans' disappointment, she added this tweet: 'In the meantime I promise I have some fun things coming up that will hopefully hold you through.'

She was as good as her word. On 27 November she staged an elaborate concert livestream called Studio 2054. It's quite possible that the name was inspired by an interview with the *Guardian*'s Laura Snapes the previous April. It was when Lipa was still uncertain about the appropriateness of releasing *Future Nostalgia* while the pandemic gathered force. Snapes wrote that Dua 'accurately concluded that her brilliant disco-wreathed anthems-in-waiting – the kind that transform kitchen tiles into a makeshift Studio 54 – might distract fans'. It was also quite possible that her younger fans knew nothing of Studio 54, the 1970s New York disco synonymous with pre-AIDS hedonism. For the curious, Google provides eye-opening pictures.

Livestreaming had come into its own during 2020, as musicians from across the pop/rock spectrum – from Billie Eilish to Linkin Park to BTS and many others – learned the ropes of virtual performance. Often, the streams showed the artist at home in a lamplit room, acoustic guitar at the ready. These intimate performances seemed the only appropriate way to perform at a time when being loud and bold would have gone against the pandemic grain; few musicians felt comfortable cranking up their amps and rocking out. Nobody wanted to raise their head above the parapet.

But Lipa was determined to live up to that tweet about 'fun things coming up'. This was to be a livestream with sky-high production values, as reflected by the $1.5 million it reportedly cost to produce. If it wasn't quite the same as watching her show from a seat in one of the arenas she now couldn't perform in, it was the closest anyone would get. Studio 2054's mission was to bring Lipa's live show to fans' laptops, and for £8.99 per view – a reasonable charge considering the complexity of the event—it did exactly what it said on the tin. There was also a £15 option giving VIP access to behind-the-scenes footage and an after-show 'party'.

But there was another, equally vital, aim. Studio 2054 wasn't just a concert; it sought to bring the nightclub experience to the viewer's living room. By November, nightlife had been closed down for eight months and nothing had been able to replace the gathering places that played a vital part in the lives of many who felt excluded or othered in the wider world. For seventy minutes, Studio 2054 would be the club, and fans' living rooms would be the dance floor.

'This is reality and fantasy exploding together,' said the official press release of Lipa's 'brand-new multi-dimensional live experience'. There's nothing like a bit of hyperbole to sell a show, yet her PR machine was entitled to boast because this livestream set a new benchmark. Officially, 5 million people watched, the largest audience for a livestream to that date, though her management estimated the true figure to be closer to 9 million, taking into account the probability that it was viewed by several people per household. Either way, it's likely that none of them felt they were settling for a not-as-good-as-reality evening in front of their devices. Because the show was ticketed, it had to be flawless, both technically – the stream couldn't be allowed to freeze – and artistically, with everything that entailed. It meant a live band was playing the songs and a dozen dancers were twirling around the stage with Dua; there were four different sets, multiple costume changes and the special guests included some pretty 'wow' names.

There was a pole-dancing FKA twigs, dueting with Lipa on 'Why Don't You Love Me?', a track the pair had started to record months earlier but hadn't finished (as of early 2023, it remains uncompleted). There was Kylie Minogue, who slung an arm around Lipa's neck as they sang 'Electricity' – a double-diva gesture that felt like the Queen of Disco recognizing the Princess of Pop. There was Belgian household name Angèle, who'd paired with Lipa on the single 'Fever', which had just hit the top of the Belgian chart.

There was Miley Cyrus, albeit not in the flesh; she and Dua had collaborated on a single called 'Prisoner' for Cyrus's new album *Plastic Hearts*, and a version of the video she and Cyrus shot for the song was aired during Studio 2054. (Sadly, the 2054 version omitted footage of Lipa driving a bus, looking for all the world like Posh Spice in the bus scene in *Spice World*.) Along the same lines, the video for the recent joint single 'Un Día' – featuring Lipa, Colombian singer J Balvin, Puerto Rican rapper Bad Bunny and producer Tainy – was also shown. Lipa sang her part live, on a 2054 stage set mocked up to look like an ornate 1950s front room, while Balvin and Bunny appeared on a black-and-white TV in the corner.

And, most starrily, there was Elton John, or at least a video stream of him beamed in from elsewhere, singing 'Rocket Man'. His sudden appearance, alone, performing one of his own songs – Lipa was offstage at this point – was incongruous (the *i* newspaper deemed his presence 'baffling') but presaged his 2021 duet with Lipa on 'Cold Heart', a mash-up of four separate John hits that reached No. 1 in Britain.

Studio 2054 was a huge endeavour, raising the bar for music livestreams. Dua, however, hadn't even wanted to do it. When the idea was presented to her in the spring of 2020, she declined, preferring to bide her time until the return of live gigs, which would have been, with the benefit of hindsight, a two-year wait. Her management suggested that instead of regarding a livestream as a poor substitute for a real gig, she think of it as a movie or a theatrical music video. Intrigued, she agreed. It would be a decision that, in its canniness, almost ranked with not delaying *Future Nostalgia*.

By late October, she reported via an Instagram live video that the preparations were rigorous. She was rehearsing six hours a day, and the process made her feel 'like I'm getting tour-ready for this one show — and it's going to be quite the spectacle'. After updating her Insta followers about the progress of Studio 2054, she remained on camera as she video-called Elton, with whom she had struck up a friendship despite at that point never having met him in the flesh. The mutual respect was clear: he was one of her idols; she was one of his favourite young singers. More than that, he 'got' her, and he got *Future Nostalgia*. She beamed as he said, 'You probably made one of the greatest albums of the year, and the thing about *Future Nostalgia* was, it caught the zeitgeist, what people wanted — they wanted something up and fun. Every track of the album is fantastic.' He, husband David Furnish and their two sons had been listening to it throughout lockdown, he told her.

High praise indeed, coming from Sir Elton ('Do you want me to address you as Sir Elton?' 'No, no, I'm always Elton. I'm never "sir'"). The reason she'd asked him to be in the Instagram update, however, was to 'interview' him about his experiences at Studio 54 – the actual club, opened in 1977 and shuttered in 1986. Elton's memories were fond. As a celebrity, he was automatically waved through by the notoriously picky doormen; inside, he had his choice of a huge dance floor or a more intimate balcony. Punters were so glamorous that many people went to the club just to see what others were wearing.

The DJs played the best of the era's dance music – 54's most celebrated period, the late seventies, coincided with a rush of groundbreaking disco, and that in itself would have ensured that Elton, a passionate follower of new music, went to the club whenever he was in New York. But there were other attractions. 'I went to look at the busboys, too – they were so cute. No shirt, [but they wore] shorts, tube socks, sneakers ...' he told a rapt Lipa. To her, this was evidence that sometimes nostalgia wasn't rose-tinted – for a short time, Studio 54 really had been, as John added, incredible. 'Incredible' was the word: the place even welcomed a horse one night, brought in as a birthday surprise for Bianca Jagger.

Some weeks after the October Insta-stream, Studio 2054's live performers, including Lipa, entered a 'quarantine house', where they lived for two weeks, rehearsing and regularly testing for Covid. It was necessary to guarantee the safety of the production but amplified the fear that life would never return to normal. Saying that, the show that resulted made the precautions worthwhile. Staged at the Printworks venue in Rotherhithe, south London, it was the first top-flight, non-socially distanced live gig in eight months, and it was a mood-elevator for all involved. The sense of liberation after nearly a year of mask-wearing and staying home can't be overstated.

Starring in the biggest global streaming event to date had significant benefits for Lipa. By taking livestreaming to a sophisticated new level, she proved herself far-sighted, while interest in the postponed Future Nostalgia tour was heightened, with *Rolling Stone* reporting that ticket sales for the tour increased by 70 per cent after 2054 aired. It also proved that her performance skills were equal to the demands of the biggest global platforms. Moreover, in the months leading up to it, she was a veritable masterclass in marketing. Once she had announced the show on 28 October, she diligently promoted it via social media right up to the day. 'STUDIO 2054 TONIGHT!!!!! SEE YOU ON THE FLIPSIDE,' she tweeted on 27 November, and in a second tweet she listed the showtimes in time zones around the world. And because it was virtual, there wouldn't be any 'Sold Out' signs tacked up on the marquee, so there was no excuse not to be there. Thus, those 5 million (or 9 million) viewers.

After the show, Studio 2054 was available to watch until 6 December for a reduced £7.50, and three months later, as the world settled into a second year of lockdown, it was re-released. Its second coming was billed as an event in its own right: it included a new documentary with backstage footage from the show and interviews with some of the guest stars. Studio 2054 & *The Story Behind the Show*, as it was titled, won Best Music Film at the UK Music Video Awards in November 2021.

A couple of days before the broadcast, Lipa received the news that she'd been nominated for six Grammy Awards, including three of the most prestigious: Album of the Year, Record of the Year ('Don't Start Now') and Song of the Year ('Don't Start Now'). The other nominations were Pop Duo/Group Performance ('Un Día'), Pop Solo Performance ('Don't Start Now') and Pop Vocal Album. Only Beyoncé got more nominations that year.

At the ceremony in March 2021, she won in just one category (Pop Vocal Album), but consider who she'd been up against: Justin Bieber, Taylor Swift, Lady Gaga and Harry Styles. Apart from rising solo star Styles, these were immensely established artists, and Lipa had bested them. While she was at it, she performed at the show – an honour only afforded to the biggest names – singing 'Levitating' and 'Don't Start Now'. Between the win and the performance, the evening signified her arrival as a bona fide major star.

The Pop Vocal Album trophy brought her total Grammys to date to three, the others having been New Artist and Dance Recording (for 'Electricity' with Silk City), both awarded at the 2019 ceremony. On that night in February 2019, she made an illuminating comment about the scope of her ambition. Interviewed backstage after winning the New Artist gong – the little gold gramophone trophy was in her hand as she answered questions – she was asked whether, in the early days, she had aspired to break America. A fair question, because the 2019 ceremony was viewed in nearly 20 million US homes, meaning Lipa had just received a substantial leg-up on that side of the Atlantic.

For most rising artists, breaking America is still high on the must-do list, despite the increasing prominence of non-anglophone acts from places never previously considered global musical hubs, like South Korea and South America. Even for those artists, however, it's enormously helpful to win over the United States. K-pop boy band BTS, for instance, were already wildly successful in Korea and Japan, but when they started chalking up a flow of No. 1 singles in America in 2020, something shifted in the way they were perceived: from that point, they were the world's biggest boy band.

For Warner Bros., America represented a big deal, and as of early 2019 Lipa's track record there was lacklustre: 'New Rules' got as far as No. 6, but none of her other singles had come anywhere close. Even the Grammy-winning 'Electricity' had only peaked at No. 62, though once 'equivalent sales' from streaming were added to 'Electricity's download sales, the track was deemed to have sold 1 million copies in the US and received platinum certification.

But for Dua, breaking America wasn't the pinnacle of her ambitions. Far from it. What she'd wanted from the outset wasn't America but the world. 'When I started, because I was living in Kosovo, I moved to London so I could do something on a global scale. My dream was trying to get my music out to as many people as possible.' A global scale – and she wasn't joking.

Chapter 12

A HOUSE IS NOT A HOME

Around the time Lipa's parents and siblings returned to England, in 2012, global success couldn't have seemed further away. The five Lipas moved into a three-bedroom ex-council flat in West Hampstead, north-west London, described by a neighbour to the *Sun* in 2019 as 'super-basic, just a few small rooms with Moroccan furniture'. It was on one of the many estates built in the capital in the 1970s and housed 'ordinary families, people from the Middle East, Somalia and Jamaica'. Around the corner were streets of classic Victorian red-brick terraced houses – the quintessential mixed London neighbourhood.

The neighbour frequently saw her coming home late at night with friends, and she was noisy about it, shouting and carousing

— or, in the neighbour's tactful words, 'in high spirits'. It was the family home until 2018, when, as the *Sun* described it, the money began to roll in. They moved to Kilburn, north London, and in January 2021 Dua bought a house in Hampstead, where the neighbours include Jimmy Carr and Boy George.

Her '£6.75 million mansion', as it was gustily characterized in the tabloids (though it wasn't a mansion, just a large-ish house on a leafy London street), has become headquarters for the entire family, including Dua when she's not in the Los Angeles house where she lives part-time. That one, in Studio City, is an open-plan redwood-and-glass structure built in 1950 and designed by John Lautner — as namechecked in *Future Nostalgia*'s title track. It would be interesting to know whether the connection influenced Lipa's decision to buy it (for $2.5 million, a relative snip in that area). It's easy to see, in any case, why she felt an affinity with the place: it's a head-turner, packing an exceptional amount of space into just six rooms, and its mid-century modern design is both elegant and restful to the eye.

Having acquired a £6.75 million house, Lipa has set about doing it up. Land is at such a premium in London that even the wealthiest owners have only one option if they want more space: they can't expand outward, so they go down. Applications for basements have soared in the past decade, as have complaints from neighbours worried about subsidence, noise and other issues. (See Robbie Williams's five-year wrangle with next-door neighbour Jimmy Page over Williams's plan to create a basement with a swimming pool and gym — former Led Zeppelin guitarist

Page objected on the grounds that vibrations from the work could damage his Grade I listed house in Holland Park, west London, but Williams eventually got permission after modifying his plans.)

Lipa filed an application in August 2021 to build a basement complex so swish it makes Williams's look like a regional leisure centre. The plans include a pool, a recording studio, a large studio waiting area, a gym, a cinema, a steam room and a 'chill-out area'. There was also a proposal to demolish a rear extension and construct a new one, as well as to add Arts and Crafts-style garden landscaping with multiple terraces, walks and plantings.

The house is in a conservation area in north London, and a neighbourhood forum objected on several grounds. One concern was that removing the original extension would be detrimental to the appearance of the house; a request to replace the ivy-covered boundary wall was also deemed inappropriate because the bricks used in the original Victorian construction are typical of the conservation area and contribute to its character. Much consternation, too, was caused by Lipa's request to fell two trees – a maple and a willow. The latter was especially valuable to the garden, said neighbours, because it may have been planted to help absorb water from an underground stream known to flow near the house.

She was granted partial permission for the renovations in October 2022, fourteen months after applying. In that time, the house's value had increased to £7 million – that was the figure the tabloids now quoted – and the additions would raise it further. In return, she had to comply with conditions relating mainly to noise. Building noise 'shall be lower than the typical existing background noise level by at least 10 decibels', the council planning officer stipulated; machinery was required to be fitted with 'anti-vibration isolators'; and the swimming-pool engine room was restricted to 28dB – the sound of a whisper. The trees she wanted to fell must be kept. (Coincidentally, at the same time Lipa received the go-ahead, Robbie Williams applied for permission to cut down trees on his own property.)

It would be pleasing if she and Boy George became friends. The singer, who has lived in his Grade II listed Gothic house since the 1980s, also had a run-in with Camden Council's planning department. His application to cut down trees and build an extension to increase the amount of natural light to his residence was refused. In December 2022, he put the house on the market for £17 million.

Dua, meanwhile, is enlarging her property portfolio. According to *Page Six*, she is building a 'sprawling multimillion-dollar mansion' in Sarandë, Albania, a city overlooking the Ionian Sea. By whatever measure you use, the new mansion will be a long way from that London council flat.

Chapter 13

THE RIGHT COLLABORATIONS

'Outside of Ariana Grande, it doesn't feel like a lot of the established A-list pop stars want to make pure pop-dance music at the moment,' radio presenter Chris Booker told *Variety* in 2018, attempting to explain Lipa's growing success in America. Booker, then at KAMP-FM in Los Angeles, noted that she was also 'doing the right collaborations — Silk City, Calvin Harris — and filling an obvious void'. Sometimes a void isn't 'obvious' until someone comes along to fill it; only then is it clear what had been missing. Lipa's pop-savviness has yielded some ear-catching team-ups, starting with the much feted 'One Kiss' (with Calvin Harris) and 'Electricity' (Silk City). Despite peaking at a lacklustre No. 26 and No. 62 respectively in the US singles chart, they were the right collaborations, with 'Electricity' winning a Grammy and 'One Kiss' selling 4 million copies as of 2022.

Having an ear for the right 'collabs', as they're known, is a basic part of the pop-star toolkit. A very good one, making optimum use of each participant's strong points, can be greater than the sum of its parts (see 'Bang Bang', the day-glo rave-up by Grande, Jessie J and Nicki Minaj that made 2014's singles chart that much brighter). An inferior one, thrown together because each party has a record to promote, bespeaks a derisory attitude toward fans, while a middling one—such as the remix of Amy Winehouse's 'You Know I'm No Good', which brought in Ghostface Killah to gild an already perfect lily—is pointless.

Lipa is generally positive about collaborations and features (the terms are often interchangeable, though 'feature' usually denotes a smaller role). She picks them judiciously, and some have been very effective team-ups: see, for instance, her slots on Sean Paul's UK Top 10 single 'No Lie' and Miley Cyrus's 'Prisoner', also a British hit. Her 2021 two-for-one with Elton John, the forlorn 'Cold Heart'—a fusion of 'Rocket Man', 'Sacrifice', 'Kiss the Bride' and 'Where's the Shoorah?' —was a big win on both sides: Lipa scored her third British No. 1, Elton his first in sixteen years. (Note also that when 'Rocket Man' was originally released in 1972, it only rocketed as far as No. 2 in the UK.) For John, a great supporter of new talent, it also brought him to the attention of Lipa's fanbase. The track was inescapable on all platforms that autumn—in America, the record label had expected it to do well on adult contemporary stations but were pleasantly surprised that it was also a hit on mainstream pop radio.

Dua had 'looked up to [John] my whole life', she told TV host Jimmy Fallon in 2022. The pair had been friends since he appeared on the Studio 2054 livestream, when he sang 'Rocket Man'. His choice of song that night might just have been influenced by Dua, who has described 'Rocket Man' as the tune she sings in her car and in the shower. A few months later, in March 2021, she performed with him at his annual pre-Oscars charity party for his Elton John AIDS Foundation (her slinky lounge take on 'Bennie and the Jets' put a whole new spin on that number). They had dinner afterward and got on famously. Several days later, while she was still in Los Angeles – she was then writing for her third album – he FaceTimed her.

She described the scene to talk-show host Stephen Colbert in 2022. She was out by the pool, wearing a bikini and a cowboy hat, about to get on with writing. Her phone rang. 'He said, "We've had this idea, we'd love to have you on this song."' It took her a nanosecond to make up her mind. Was he joking? Of *course* she would do it. Elton insisted she listen to the song first. No need, said Dua – she would 100 per cent sing the song. But he refused to take it any further until she'd heard it. She listened; of the four John songs used to concoct 'Cold Heart' – the remixing and moulding had been done by Australian trio Pnau – 'Rocket Man' was the most prominent element.

To Lipa, it was fate – she was meant to do it. She told Colbert she felt she'd manifested it. 'Manifesting' is a practice based on the belief that a person can influence events by focusing on what they want. The concept has existed for centuries but went mainstream with the publication of the 2006 book *The Secret*, which has been highly popular with celebrities. Colbert, kind but a little sceptical, asked, 'You drew him into your life by reading *The Secret*?' 'Yes,' she said, then laughed sheepishly, aware of how it sounded. Nevertheless, she was convinced that their collaboration had come about at least partly because she strongly wanted it to.

John was then recording *The Lockdown Sessions* — an album of collaborations that would be released in October 2021 and reach No. 1 in Britain. 'Cold Heart' ended up as the record's first track, so the Dua/John interface was unmissable. Reviews of the song were mixed: PopMatters thought it was 'cut and paste', but the *Independent* liked its 'tendon-twanging freshness', and Renowned for Sound deemed it 'a song the world never knew it needed'. More than that, Renowned heard a modern anthem in the making, citing its use of several of John's most celebrated songs, Lipa's pop input and Pnau's house-inflected mixing.

By that point, Lipa and John were firm friends, and even before 'Cold Heart' she had been a recipient of his generosity. Elton is known for his munificence toward people he likes, and so it was with Lipa. The night they had performed at the pre-Oscars show, he'd invited her to his hotel room before the show. He wanted to give her 'something special' that he owned: a vintage diamond set in a gold band. It was so exquisite, she told *Marie Claire*, that she never takes it off: 'I feel like it brings me luck.'

Despite her open-mindedness about collaborations, Lipa gets more requests than she can accept. In some cases, as with rapper Kid Cudi, the problem has been timing; in September 2022 he said that he'd suggested that they work together, but she wanted to spend the rest of the year chilling. He added hopefully: 'Dua, I'm ready whenever you're ready, baby.' In other cases, she just doesn't feel a connection, and at those points she'll tell the other artist, no matter how successful they are. Sydney-based electro-producer Flume, maker of two albums that topped the Australian chart, sent Lipa two separate feature pitches, but she declined both. Her kind but straightforward reply was: 'These are great but they're not going with my vibe right now.'

Her vibe was much more attuned to artists like Megan Thee Stallion. Lipa and the San Antonio-born rapper were mutual fans, and some admirers had long thought they would be a perfect pairing on a track. One fan even made a remix of 'Levitating', slipping in a Megan rap from the song 'Fkn Around' and posted it on Twitter. Megan heard it and decided it sounded so good, it would be foolish if she and Lipa didn't get together and make a song of their own. 'I love Dua, she's so fire,' she wrote on Instagram. Lipa replied, 'I love you @TheeStallion let's get it!!!!'

Once they'd agreed to work together, Megan tasked herself with finding the right beat before pursuing things further. Producer OG Parker sent her an incredibly infectious instrumental snippet, and that was it – there was the beat. She and Lipa then wrote the song (Clarence Coffee, Sarah Hudson, Koz, Nija Charles and Parker are also credited), which they titled 'Sweetest Pie', and it was a cracker. A twinkling, Miami bass-style track, it had the catchiest chorus since 'Levitating', and the contrast between Lipa's silken vocal and Megan's tumbling flow worked just fine.

Both women are at the top of their abilities, representing different scenes but working in harmony.

With that said, as loveable as the tune is, the lyric is predictable. As a songwriter, Megan often produces verses brimming with sexual explicitness, which is the case on 'Sweetest Pie', although she enrobes them in frequently hilarious similes. Lipa's verses, meanwhile, are a rather limp invitation to taste her sweet pie. Together, it's a bit sexy-by-numbers, but the words are eminently redeemed by the rest of the tune and that abundantly catchy chorus.

Megan also came up with the concept for the haunting video. 'Haunting' means, in this case, that it could keep you awake at night, with a horror storyline that roves from a spider crawling down Lipa's face to a scene showing the two women about to be burned at the stake in front of a mob of cheering men. Luckily, the Dua/Megan superpowers are functioning, and they turn the situation around, burning the men instead and burying them in ash.

For all its merits, when 'Sweetest Pie' was released in March 2022, it only reached No. 15 in the US Top 100 — which did at least make it Lipa's sixth Top 20 single there — and in the UK got only as far as No. 31. More was expected; after all, it was Lipa's first single release in Britain since 'Cold Heart' topped the chart five months before, and as a collaboration partner Megan was as A-list as it got. The two performed the song on several American dates of the Future Nostalgia tour, and the fan reaction to Megan when she imperiously glided down a flight of stairs to join Dua was everything either could have wanted. But, as stated earlier, sometimes a song just doesn't connect.

In the early stages of Lipa's career it was tempting to do whatever features or collabs she was offered for the sake of the exposure, but that had to be weighed against the drawbacks of choosing one that wasn't the right fit. 'When features aren't done correctly, they don't represent who you are as an artist and you get a bit lost,' she told *NME* in 2017. Having said that, even she has sometimes made the wrong call: as featured artist on Wale's 'My Love' (2017), she's overshadowed by the powerhouse American MC, while a 2018 duet with Andrea Bocelli, 'If Only', casts her as the earnest duet partner who doesn't quite match up to Bocelli's opera-trained power. As the song progresses, Lipa works up to a peak of Celine Dion-esque passion that brings to mind Dion's 'My Heart Will Go On'. It's impressive but so antithetical to Lipa's normal style that it's boggling to hear. It came out as a single but failed to chart, despite support from Radio 2. On the brighter side, it also appeared on Bocelli's pop-classical album *Si*, which reached the top of the charts in both the UK and the US, thus introducing Lipa to an audience that might not have heard her before (Ariana Grande, Ed Sheeran and other major pop names have also collaborated with Bocelli and presumably achieved similar crossover success).

What follows is a list of Lipa's best collaborations, and a couple that arguably don't quite work.

GOOD

'Kiss and Make Up' – Dua Lipa, featuring Blackpink (2018)

Getting together with the K-pop girl group Blackpink could only have one outcome: a fizzy banger. Sung half in English, half in Korean, it's a party-starter, but it wasn't pushed much when released for download and streaming, so it's been overlooked, though it did do well in Europe and the Far East. Lipa and the group – currently one of the world's biggest girl bands – met when Lipa was playing in Seoul. 'Kiss and Make Up', which had been written eighteen months earlier but lain dormant since because Lipa hadn't considered it a solo number, suddenly came to mind as a track they could record together. It was hindered by being released a month after 'Electricity' – Dua's double-header with Silk City – and by the fact that the two singles were on different labels. 'Kiss and Make Up' came out on Lipa's label, Warner Bros. Records, while 'Electricity' was handled by Silk City's Columbia/ Sony Records. Though the track reached No. 1 in Malaysia and Singapore, 'Electricity' was the bigger hit due to it being plugged in America and Britain and getting the lion's share of attention.

'Electricity' – Silk City and Dua Lipa, featuring Diplo and Mark Ronson (2018)

Lipa files this in the 'fun song' category – it's a sleek house throwback that captures the electric sensation of falling in love and it 'sending electric messages all up and down your spine'. Diplo and Ronson had met as young DJs twenty years before and formed Silk City in 2018 as an homage to the cities that were in the dance-music vanguard in the eighties: Chicago, Detroit, London, Paris. Too young to have experienced the first wave of dance, Lipa nonetheless had an instinctive understanding of Diplo and Ronson's idea and knew that 'Electricity' needed the immersive warmth she often brings to her vocals. The tune is a grower rather than an instant banger. On first listen, it sounds like a generic eighties dance track, but – rather like good wine – it needs time to breathe. Lipa's vocal is foregrounded, while the piano backing subtly builds to a hands-in-the-air crescendo. Meanwhile, in the video ...

The Bradley & Pablo-directed clip switches between scenes of Lipa partying with friends in a Manhattan loft during a blackout, and glimpses of Ronson and Diplo, who are trying to get to the party but are stuck in the lift. It's a broiling summer's night and the lights have gone out all over the city, but Dua and her friends' frenzied dancing creates 'electricity' of its own and the lights flicker back on. They dance till dawn – but Ronson and Diplo spend the night in the lift, futilely banging on the walls. The last moment of the clip tunes in on the lift again, where the pair are listlessly sitting on the floor, having discovered that even super-producers can't ace their way out of a stuck elevator and temperatures in the nineties Fahrenheit. Both video and song are tremendous fun, and Lipa was especially pleased with the video, which was a turning point 'in terms of confidence'. It was the first time she had been in front of a camera and not been self-conscious about onlookers' opinions.

'One Kiss' – Calvin Harris and Dua Lipa (2018)

Here's the recipe for Britain's biggest single of 2018: Calvin Harris supplies the Eurodance beats, Lipa the husky invitation to see where a kiss might lead. 'One Kiss' spent eight weeks at No. 1 and by 2022 had amassed 1.5 billion streams. The Official Charts Company named it 2018's 'biggest single' based on a combination of audio streams, downloads and video streams, which equated to 1.57 million sales. It also won the British Single of the Year award at the 2019 Brits. Given a compatible female vocalist and a fair wind, Harris can do this kind of catchy nineties-house thing in his sleep – see also 'We Found Love' with Rihanna and 'Outside' with Ellie Goulding – but on 'One Kiss' he and Lipa discovered a synergy that bounced it to the top of everyone's summer-listening playlists. From this, they also developed a lasting friendship that finds Lipa going to his studio to get his opinion on songs she's just recorded.

'Demeanor' – Pop Smoke, featuring Dua Lipa (2021)

One of the millions who had a soft spot for 'One Kiss' was Brooklyn rapper Pop Smoke, who tweeted a snippet of himself wafting his arms to the tune as it played on a car sound system. When Smoke was killed by burglars in 2020, he'd recorded part of 'Demeanor', intending it to be used on the album *Exodus* by the revered DMX (who himself died before *Exodus* was completed). Instead, Pop's vocal ended up on a single under his own name, with Lipa as featured vocalist. Sparse and tense, 'Demeanor' feels like a demo. It could well *be* a demo; it consists of nothing more than a drill beat, Pop's coiled-spring verses and Dua's imperious pop chorus. As on *Future Nostalgia*'s title track, she again identifies as a 'female alpha', urging Smoke not to underestimate her because she has the 'meaner' demeanour. The two make such an unlikely musical couple that the only word for this song is 'weird', though that weirdness – the stylistic clash – is also what sells it.

It's difficult to establish exactly when Lipa recorded her part, or, indeed, how she got involved (reportedly, Pop's first choice was Bruno Mars). The credits list her as a co-writer, but it's not even clear whether they recorded together or if she added her verse after Smoke's death. Having Lipa on the track broadened its appeal, sending it to No. 14 in the UK chart. In America, it stalled outside the Top 75, but Smoke's posthumous album *Faith*, which contained the single and was released the same week, hit No. 1.

The track's visual, incidentally, is a must-watch. Set in a Bavarian castle, it has Lipa in a Queen Anne-era ballgown, gliding past an orgiastic banquet, while the late Pop is represented by a ghostly puff of smoke.

'Homesick' – Dua Lipa with Chris Martin (2017)

Not an 'official' collaboration – Martin's name doesn't appear on the tracklisting on *Dua Lipa*'s back cover – 'Homesick' is one of Lipa's prettiest moments. It's the closing track on the album and one of her few unabashed ballads. Not only is it a ballad, it's a piano ballad. Usually the province of downtempo singer-songwriters, for Lipa it's a million miles from her usual uptempo bops. She'd long wanted to work with Martin and sent him some unreleased tracks via a mutual friend, hoping he'd like them enough to want to write a song with her. A joint writing session was all she was expecting, but when they met up in the Coldplay leader's Malibu studio and sketched out several melodies together, she felt they had an instinctive artistic understanding.

She was gobsmacked to be sitting in his studio, listening as he played the melodies on piano. She told *NME* that she was thinking, 'This is the guy you went to see at Glastonbury. What's happening to me? This is crazy.' Thus emboldened, she asked him to sing on the track. But that wasn't until their second writing session; during the first, she and Martin spent several hours discussing music and what she was hoping for with this collaboration.

Martin liked the unreleased songs mentioned above, which included 'New Rules', so much that he danced in the studio, then questioned her closely about them. She showed him ideas she'd had for her second and third albums – this, of course, was before she'd even released the first – and he was deeply impressed by her creativity and ambition. All right, then, he said, 'Let's write one for your [still uncompleted debut] album.' Before they began to write, Lipa had already come up with the title 'Homesick', and when they sat down and started in earnest, she fleshed out the meaning behind the title. As previously discussed, it was about the yearning brought on when she spent time in warm, sunny places far from London – such as Los Angeles, where she was often obliged to go for work. More than anything, she misses London rain when she's in LA, and on the infrequent occasions that Los Angeles sees rainfall, her yearning for home is even sharper.

On their second (and final) studio session, they'd agreed that Lipa would sing and Martin would play piano. If they'd left it that way, 'Homesick' still would have been beautiful. But as they proceeded, she realized that what the track needed was another voice harmonizing with hers. He demurred; she 'begged' until he agreed. Lipa is delicate and vulnerable on her solo verses, and when Martin joins in at one minute thirty seconds, their voices meld warmly. Too often, piano ballads are maudlin or drippy; this one, however, is simply lovely, and as a last-minute addition to *Dua Lipa*, it closes the album on a soft, contemplative note.

'Sugar' (remix) – Brockhampton, featuring Dua Lipa (2020)

Another unexpected-but-winning feature was this remixed version of a 2019 single by 'the world's greatest boy band' – Brockhampton's own description, though they weren't a 'boy band' in the usual sense. The Texas thirteen-piece, who split up in 2022, had acquired a dedicated and vocal following, but for all their idiosyncratic charm – they 'aimed to fuse Odd Future's gonzo spirit with pop choruses', said the *Guardian* – they hadn't had a hit single. Boy bands, gonzo or not, live or die on their hit-count. But help was on the way in the form of Lipa, who had always liked their music: what better way for the band to get chart recognition than to work with the UK's biggest female pop name? Their silky R&B ballad 'Sugar' had been out for a couple of months by this point and was starting to take off as a dance on TikTok; working with Lipa could push it even further.

They approached her manager with a view to getting her onto

a remix, and she accepted immediately. Her only condition was that they do it together, all of them in the studio, rather than – as is the case with many collaborations – remotely. She was already in Los Angeles, where the band were based, and met them a few days later (it was late January 2020, and she remembers the time and place because she'd been to the Grammy Awards and was hungover the next day, so she met them the day after that). Their two-hour writing session yielded the verse that Lipa sings on the record; she took it home to London, re-recorded her vocal, and sent it back to Brockhampton. Thanks to Lipa, TikTok and 'Sugar' simply being a good song, the band got the big record they were after – 2 million 'track equivalent' sales – while it benefited Lipa, too, by keeping her visible in the run-up to the release of *Future Nostalgia*.

The remix was highly praised for being more than just a remix: rather than simply tacking Lipa's verse onto the song, the arrangement was changed and her vocal dipped in and out throughout. For three minutes, she was the fourteenth member of Brockhampton, making her presence felt.

'Levitating' (The Blessed Madonna remix) – Dua Lipa, featuring Madonna and Missy Elliott (2020)

This collaboration trumps everything else in Lipa's catalogue for sheer star-power. The already brilliant 'Levitating' was given a makeover by American DJ/producer The Blessed Madonna – no relation to Madonna the singer – who sped up the beats and ramped up the electronics. What was simply a supremely catchy pop track became a glittering disco event with the same clubby,

1980s feel as Madonna's 2012 album *MDNA*. All Lipa had to do was get Madonna to sing on it and Missy Elliott to rap.

Lipa didn't think it would be possible to rope in Madonna, because, well, she's Madonna. She hesitantly asked manager Ben Mawson whether he thought it was too crazy an idea to approach her. He thought they might as well try – and Madonna said yes. Shortly after that (this was around June 2020), the two vocalists had a twenty-minute phone conversation that ranged from boyfriends to politics to 'Levitating' itself. Lipa was nervous before they spoke, but Madonna surpassed her expectations; she was 'fun and bubbly', Lipa told *Attitude*, and best of all, she loved the song.

Elliott, too, was thrilled to be involved, telling *NME*: 'I am humbly grateful that Dua asked me to be part of this record because I am a fan of her work.' Elliott might have been grateful, but Lipa was nothing less than over the moon. She phoned Elliott to discuss the particulars and afterward told Apple Music's Zane Lowe: 'She really just does stuff that she really believes in, so that I felt it was such a massive compliment [to] me.' Lipa sent Elliott The Blessed Madonna's remix, and she loved it: 'I was like, "Ooh, this is fire!"' She recorded her part straightaway. Her verse was 'tastefully naughty', said Radio.com, which is to say suggestive without explicitness, bar one line about the cartoon character Betty Boop. Her flow was no less fiery for the passage of time – this was prime Missy.

The Blessed Madonna (offstage name: Marea Stamper) stitched the three vocal parts into a glossy disco-EDM hybrid. It was 'a colossal pop moment', according to *Clash* magazine –

or a 'ludicrous pop pileup', said the *Guardian*. More than that, it was a gargantuan assertion that women together are powerful. *Billboard*, in fact, referred to the four as 'the power quartet'.

Careful listening might be required to recognize Madonna's voice in the mix; surprisingly, it doesn't sound very different from Lipa's. And more confusingly still, in the video, in which Madonna doesn't appear, Lipa lip syncs the former's lines. But that's her on the second verse and on some of the ad libs.

The song was created for *Club Future Nostalgia*, a remix album Lipa and her management dreamed up as a hedonistic reaction to the Covid lockdown. It was a companion piece to the *Future Nostalgia* LP, an album that would live alongside it, and it was recorded as a seamless, vintage-style mixtape. Stamper's job, as executive producer, was to oversee the editing, commission other remixes and pull all the features together into a fifty-minute club mix. And it had to be done secretly, because Lipa was concerned that it would leak, as *Future Nostalgia* had. Stamper worked alone in her attic studio in east London, and in August 2020, just five months after the release of *Future Nostalgia*, *Club Future Nostalgia* was ready: seventeen remixes that Lipa guaranteed would take the party up a notch. Not every fan was enthusiastic at the idea that *FN* had been tinkered with; some were downright hostile, because in their view the tracks were perfect, and to change them was to ruin them. 'It's going to be a new thing, so there's going to be a moment of shock, and that is totally OK,' Stamper told an Idolator interviewer.

Though the LP debuted at No. 1 in *Billboard*'s Dance/Electronic

Albums chart on 12 September 2020, reviews were mixed. The 'shock' Stamper foresaw didn't materialize, but some critics had reservations about certain tracks, with Madonna and Elliott's hook-up mentioned more than once. Pitchfork's Owen Myers, for instance, thought the two were 'more charismatic when they teamed up for a GAP commercial [in 2003]'; AllMusic felt it didn't quite '[hit] the highs ... targeted'. Yet AllMusic's overall verdict was positive: 'Fans who can't get enough of [*Future Nostalgia*] will find *Club Future Nostalgia* to be an absolute blast.' Given Lipa's intention that the remix album should serve as a gift to fans and a reminder of the real-life dance floors many were missing, it's hard to disagree that it was exactly that.

'Lost in Your Light' — Dua Lipa, featuring Miguel (2017)

The only collaboration on *Dua Lipa* was this, an unabashed smoocher with Californian R&B prince Miguel. He had been on her wishlist of prospective duet partners; Lipa loved his work so much that when they met for a single day in a Los Angeles studio, she 'was [fangirling] a bit'. Perhaps that's why she describes their sumptuous electropop duet as 'one of the happier songs from the album'. The rest of the LP might fall into her 'dance-crying' category, but 'Lost in Your Light' is a giddy expression of infatuation with a new person — no crying necessary.

Unusually for a Lipa collaboration, it's a proper duet and takes full advantage of the fact the singers happen to harmonize dreamily together. Their joined voices on the chorus are among the best moments on *Dua Lipa*. Some critics felt that by treating the song as a duet of equals, Lipa watered down her personality, but that view fails to acknowledge that, sometimes, two voices just sound great together and that's all that matters.

'Prisoner' — Miley Cyrus, featuring Dua Lipa (2020)

Cyrus and Lipa are a pop dream team — mutually respectful alpha females, both handy with a pop tune and both dedicated to making 'Prisoner' as much of a bop as possible. It's on Cyrus's 2020 album *Plastic Hearts* and was also added to *The Moonlight Edition* — Lipa's 2021 reissue of *Future Nostalgia*, which contained new songs. It came about after they'd already recorded several tracks together and rejected them for not feeling like 'a true partnership' (Cyrus's words). Lipa insisted they press on until they'd written something that expressed their individuality while also capturing their chemistry as a duo. 'Prisoner' is it.

Technically, Cyrus takes more ownership of the song, which alludes to her relationship with her ex-husband, Liam Hemsworth. She sings the intro, pre-chorus and one of the verses herself, but Lipa's smoky mezzo-soprano shines on their shared verses. Though Cyrus is a gritty rocker at heart — at least, *Plastic Hearts* is a rock album, with guest spots from Billy Idol and Joan Jett — and Lipa a disco queen, they mesh. Between them, they fashioned a glam-rock party tune that could have come from the catalogues of Jett or Pat Benatar, and they pay tribute to Olivia Newton-John in the chorus, with its interpolation of her 1981 smash 'Physical'. Their partnership elevates 'Prisoner' to the classic-banger tier and gives the accompanying video, in which they play carousing vampires, a shot of caution-to-the-wind hilarity. The video became mildly controversial when some people accused the pair, who spend much of their screen time writhing together in a bar, of queer-baiting, but in the view of most critics it was 'packed with attitude', as *NME* put it.

'Un Día (One Day)' – Dua Lipa, J Balvin, Bad Bunny and Tainy (2020)

It wasn't especially surprising that Lipa collaborated with the giants of reggaeton – Balvin, Bad Bunny and producer Tainy – on a song sung half in Spanish. Naturally given to exploring different genres, Lipa probably would have come to reggaeton eventually anyway – and here she is with its undisputed kings, more than holding her own on a melancholy ballad. The surprise was that 'Un Día' was nominated for a Grammy in 2021 in the Best Pop Duo/ Group Performance category, competing with Justin Bieber, Taylor Swift, BTS and a Lady Gaga/Ariana Grande team-up (which won).

It's not that the track wasn't worthy of the nod; it was. But a Grammy nomination tends to reflect not just the quality of a song but its sales success, and outside Spanish-speaking countries 'Un Día's chart positions were disappointing (No. 63 on the *Billboard* Hot 100; No. 72 in Britain – though it did top *Billboard*'s Hot Latin and Latin Airplay charts). The Latin American record industry is recognized by its own ceremony, the Latin Grammys, which has awarded Balvin and Bunny several trophies each in the past few years. Recently, however, the English-speaking music industry has been taking a broader view of non-anglophone music due to the rocketing popularity of artists like Balvin and Bunny and

K-pop bands like BTS. It seems likely that 'Un Día's nomination was part of an initiative to 'normalize' languages other than English in the US industry. There is also the fact that Lipa, a non-Spanish speaker – 'but I bloody wish I did' understand Spanish, she once said – contributed her verses in English, making the song bilingual.

Lipa immediately wanted to get involved when Balvin contacted her at the end of 2018 about the track he was making with Tainy and Bad Bunny. In Latin America, Lipa was mainly known to people who followed British pop. Teaming up with the two biggest stars in the region would change that, perhaps even helping her ascend to *chica principal del pop* ('main pop girl') status. The Latino artists, in their turn, would be introduced to Lipa's fans, and Balvin, hopefully, would find himself in the UK chart for the first time since 2017, when the single 'Mi Gente' reached No. 5.

Lipa hinted at the collaboration in January 2019, posting a picture of herself and Balvin and the ambiguous comment, '2019 is all about making new friends. Overdue link up @jbalvin.' By then, the song had already been recorded, and there was a tentative plan to put it on *Oasis*, a Balvin/Bunny joint album scheduled for that June. But Lipa was reluctant to release any new music then; her next 'era' was slated to begin in November with the unveiling of 'Don't Start Now', and making a new song available months earlier in June would confuse things. In the end, it came out in July 2020, in a gap between 'Hallucinate' and 'Levitating (Remix)', and Balvin added it to his 2021 album *Jose*.

Some fans were disappointed that this meeting of genres

from different worlds – Dua's pop-house in one corner, Balvin and Bunny's reggaeton rhythms in the other – didn't produce an uptempo summer dance track. It was exactly the opposite; its mid-paced, brooding nostalgia militated against dancing – this was the kind of record that compelled the listener to sit down with a glass of wine and mistily remember the one who got away. Lipa's voice, chilled and contemplative, fit the mood well, and her verses complemented Balvin's rap-singing and rapper Bad Bunny's high-speed flow.

'No Lie' – Sean Paul, featuring Dua Lipa (2016)

Lipa and Jamaican rapper Sean Paul had a rollicking time on this dancehall/R&B number, though Paul knew little about her before they collaborated. Its hook, written by Emily Warren who would go on to co-write 'New Rules' and 'Don't Start Now', was so grabby that Paul thought Warren herself might be the perfect person to sing it on the record. Instead, Warren recruited Lipa. She played her the song over lunch, and Lipa loved it. 'I knew they were looking for a feature, and I [thought], "Oh, this would be really cool," [but] I didn't think anything would come of it,' Lipa said in a Vevo 'Behind the Scenes' video.

It turned out that if Warren couldn't do it, Paul wanted an up-and-coming singer, so she was in with a shout. A few weeks later, Lipa got the nod. She was delighted, having been a Paul fan since he'd guested on Beyoncé's song 'Baby Boy' (Lipa was then in Year 3). Paul, for his part, hadn't heard much of Lipa's music, but she recorded a demo of 'No Lie' and her ease with it convinced him she was right for the record. Her voice was 'so very sensual', he told Idolator.

The track is a straight-down-the-line lust song, conveying Paul's admiration for a woman who looks like a goddess and exudes 'phatness' (he does attempt to balance the appearance-based compliments by adding that she's brainy, too). Lipa's high-wattage choruses, sung in a slight Jamaican accent, assure Paul that she's up for a 'lit' time tonight. There's no subtlety here, no attempt to do anything more than have the best time possible. 'No Lie' reached the UK Top 10 and its video surpassed 1 billion views in April 2022.

'High' – Whethan and Dua Lipa (2018)

'High' is a relative obscurity, if 'obscurity' can be applied to a song that's been streamed 122 million times. Despite the numbers, it's one of Lipa's lesser-known songs: it was commissioned for the *Fifty Shades Freed* soundtrack (it's heard in a scene where Anastasia washes Christian Grey's hair, and the song's haunting sparseness ratchets up the tension considerably), but it never got the traction enjoyed by the soundtrack's lead single, 'For You', sung by Liam Payne and Rita Ora. It was popular enough to reach No. 12 in the *Billboard* dance chart, and Lipa included it in the setlist of her Self-Titled tour, but it's still a track that only dedicated fans know.

Made with Chicago teen-prodigy producer Whethan (he was working with Skrillex by the time he was seventeen and was just eighteen when he collaborated with Lipa), 'High' is one of Lipa's barest songs, and all the more striking for it. Whethan concocts a barely-there electronic soundscape, against which Lipa's cracked, bluesy tone is powerfully eerie. It starts with her humming in a gospel-ish way, setting up the expectation that this is different from the usual Lipa song. Then she flows into the electro-blues body of the song, which – dark and burning – is unlike anything she had done before. While *Fifty Shades Freed*, last of the *Fifty Shades* trilogy, has been roundly panned, 'High' conveys the film's carnality far more effectively. If it's similar to anything in her catalogue, it would be her version of Etta James's 'I'd Rather Go Blind', her teenage take on the blues.

LESS GOOD

'My Love' – Wale, featuring Major Lazer, Wizkid and Dua Lipa (2017)

Washington DC rapper Wale stacked this song with guests – not just Lipa but Afrobeats hero Wizkid and electro-dancehall outfit Major Lazer. With a VIP list like that, someone was going to end up being overshadowed by the more dominant artists, and that was Lipa.

Diplo, the most high-profile member of Major Lazer (he would later produce 'Electricity', Lipa's link-up with Silk City), thought Lipa would be a good fit for 'My Love's mash-up of dance, Afrobeats and hip-hop, and he texted her saying he had a song she might like. Lipa had a long-unfulfilled wish to work with Diplo and was ready to listen to whatever he sent. The track, when it arrived, already had Wale's and Wizkid's voices on it; she went into the studio and 'vocaled the song', sent it back and was thrilled when Wale gave it the thumbs-up. 'I was like, "Cool, let's do it,"' she recounted to Complex.

The finished track, which appeared on Wale's album *Shine*, is a sunny tune seemingly created to soundtrack beach parties – fittingly, the video was filmed on a Southern California beach and is fine enough. But Lipa's contribution, appealingly husky as it is, pales in comparison to Wale's and Wizkid's exuberance. 'My Love' would have done just fine without her; for once, she was surplus to requirements.

The track, described by Complex as the album's 'standout cut', was streamed 90 million times on Spotify, but the album itself wasn't a sales hit. It reached a US chart peak of No. 16 – a disappointment for an artist whose last two records had debuted at No. 1. Two years later, in a Twitter discussion, Wale reflected, '"Fine Girl" [another *Shine* cut] was a year and a half too early ...' A fan replied, 'And "My Love" never got its due.' Wale's answer to that perhaps acknowledges the power Lipa had accrued by 2019: 'I'm like one Dua Lipa post away from creeping on a gold record perhaps.'

'Physical' (Mark Ronson remix) – Dua Lipa, featuring Gwen Stefani (2020)

Sometimes an idea that looks good on paper fizzles when exposed to real life. This remix, from *Club Future Nostalgia*, contains the ingredients of a banger – Gwen Stefani, Mark Ronson and one of Lipa's most energized songs – but the result is one of the album's less distinctive tracks. Lipa had been a Stefani fan since the day in 2005 when the latter's hit 'Hollaback Girl' planted itself in the nine-year-old Dua's consciousness. Fifteen years later, she was in a position to meet Stefani on an artist-to-artist footing: Lipa asked her for permission to use a sample from 'Hollaback Girl' in a remix of 'Hallucinate', which was granted. Although Marea Stamper was by now putting the finishing touches on *CFN*, Lipa thought it couldn't hurt to see whether Stefani was interested in singing on the album herself.

It happened that Mark Ronson had remixed 'Physical' for *CFN*, and Stefani had heard and loved it. Shortly afterward, Stamper got a call from Lipa. 'I know we're done, but Gwen wants to be on the record. Do we have time? Can we make it happen?' Stamper hastily made a verse for her, and 'Physical', which had been scheduled as a simple Ronson remix with Lipa's vocal on it, was now Lipa, Stefani and Ronson. The problem: Ronson's mix turned the tune into a race, with Lipa speeding up to keep pace with it. Stefani, meanwhile, is a pop singer who's not a natural dance vocalist, and her vocal (she's on the second verse) is sweet and coy rather than exuberant and celebratory, as the song demands. Reviews were mixed; one critic simply wondered why they hadn't done the 'obvious' thing and sampled Olivia Newton-John's 'Physical' — same name, very different song.

— — —

Lipa has had a good run of collaborations so far. They've been so varied that it's impossible to predict what she'll try next; she's as likely to make a wistful piano ballad with a major rock star or a drill track with an American MC as she is a more 'typical' dance-pop concoction with like-minded friends, such as Mark Ronson and Diplo. That leaves the door open for intriguing hook-ups in her forthcoming third-album era.

Chapter 14

THAT VOICE

T hanks to TV singing competitions such as the *X Factor* and *The Voice*, the mainstream idea of how a pop voice should sound has changed. Characterful, 'flawed' voices are out of fashion, with the odd exception – Lewis Capaldi or Billie Eilish, say. The emphasis has shifted to power and use of the upper range. The idea is not to sing but, as former *Voice* judge Jessie J once put it, to *sang*. Sanging sometimes involves belting – using the lower (chest) voice to strengthen the top (head) voice for a jolt of maximum energy: Adele can belt, as can, surprisingly, Dave Grohl. But sanging's defining characteristics are melisma – the ululating sound of one syllable warbled at length – and use of the upper register. The booming power of it conveys emotion, or at least that's the idea.

Ariana Grande and Celine Dion embody the talent-show idea of what a pop voice should be, while Lipa does not. She's a mezzo-soprano; they're lyric sopranos and characteristically use their powerful upper registers. Dion and Grande are unsurpassable forces of nature (and sparing in their use of melisma), yet they're the impossible standard to which thousands of vocalists, both female and male, aspire. (Note that male vocals are also often higher pitched in today's pop; see Justin Bieber, Shawn Mendes and most members of BTS, for starters.) Compared to Grande and many of this decade's A-listers, Lipa is the odd one out. As a mezzo-soprano, her natural register is at the lower end of the scale — the end where a voice becomes 'darker' as it descends in pitch. While she has worked to expand her upper range, she'll always be more comfortable further down. That's her trademark: the rounded, husky tone that sets her apart from most women making pop records today. Hearing her live confirms how atypical she is. She might not have the melodic runs or 'technique', but her burnished resonance is one of pop's most singular sounds.

She's unusual enough that American voice coach Hannah Bayles, 'reacting' online to her performance of 'Levitating' at the 2021 Grammys, was transfixed. She approved of Lipa's control of her chest voice, which is a crucial bit of self-care for singers, who otherwise risk damage to their vocal cords. She was impressed that she went no higher than a B. But most of the 'reaction' consisted of open-mouthed astonishment at Lipa's charisma. 'What a pop star!' she cried. Lipa certainly is.

There's some debate about whether she really is a mezzo.

Some believe that her low voice and timbre make her an alto, others that she's a 'criminally underdeveloped lyric soprano', in the words of one fan. Her chest voice, when mixed with higher notes, is warm, however, and the consensus is that she's a mezzo.

Knowing her voice well also gives Dua full control of her tone. If she didn't have this – a typical problem for people with strong lower ranges – the fullness could become too loud. Ascending a series of notes, a singer might be tempted to hit each one with increasing power, blasting their way to the top. Lipa, on the other hand, reins in the power as she climbs; her big voice enables her to ascend effortlessly, but she never blares. When she reaches the top, she's able to deftly switch from dark to light, with the occasional squeak of air coming through. Los Angeles-based vocal coach Tristan Paredes calls it 'taming the beast', or in other words controlling the force of her tone to avoid 'getting shouty'. Shoutiness is a trait found among people with strong voices, but one that Lipa resists.

Critiquing her cover of Etta James's 'I'd Rather Go Blind' from the 2017 EP *Live Acoustic*, Paredes is wowed by her open-throated resonance. 'She's intuitively good with her voice,' he says, pointing out that when she reaches the high-pitched peak of the song there's not a trace of the nasal shrillness that can attend when a singer goes full throttle in their upper register.

On the subject of her upper register, the English singer and coach Lisa Grand has praised Lipa's 'smiling' delivery of brighter songs like 'Don't Start Now'. The upbeat 'brightness' of the melody literally forces a smile as she sings, in turn opening the sound of the notes. Grand also singles out the harmonies achieved with her backing vocalists. The best place to hear them is on the *Tiny Desk (Home)* concert broadcast in December 2020, where the acoustic setting makes it easy to appreciate the blend and tuning of the voices. Lipa has four singers in the living room with her — Naomi Scarlett, Ciara O'Connor, Izzy Chase and Matthew Allen — and Grand was impressed by the warmth and 'fatness' they created. They're so blended that they could be one rich voice rather than four. One thing particularly stood out for Grand: Lipa's involvement with her group. She wasn't a singer standing in front of a backing quartet; she was part of the ensemble.

Lipa thrives when singing *with* other people—which isn't to say that she won't make a solo acoustic album one day, just to shock everyone — but she truly comes alive when singing *for* others. For an audience, in other words, whether in a venue or on a TV stage. True, she had a tricky initiation into live performance, circa 2016, when she played pubs and clubs and spent every night standing on a tiny stage, wondering what to say to the people who'd come to see her. However, confidence is a Lipa attribute that's rarely in short supply, and within a year she found the courage to get up there and put on a capital-S Show.

Even if her 2017 budget didn't allow for the bells-and-whistles productions that would follow when she became an arena act, she was assertive and positive when performing. This was *her* stage, these people had paid to be there and that was enough to fire her up. On top of that, the live work gradually honed her vocals. Through consistent gigging, she'd found the spot where everything gelled – voice, attitude, look – but without the vocal skills, she would have been just another pop starlet. By the middle of 2017, when *Dua Lipa* came out, Lipa was able to turn up in front of a crowd and know she would sound warm and pitch-perfect – not dissimilar to the way she did on the record. That's not to imply that she mimed on stage, then or now. She didn't and doesn't. Lipa is simply one of the few singers who can cut it as easily live as in a recording studio. The point is, given an appreciative audience, she's up there with the best.

A medley she performed at the 2021 Brit Awards is as good a demonstration as any of her live ability. It started with a pre-recorded segment of her swooning through 'Love Again' on a moving London Tube train and progressed to her bursting onto the stage at the awards singing 'Physical', followed by excerpts from most of *Future Nostalgia*. Every syllable was live. The choreography, which packed in a high-octane twerking segment, was demanding enough that she should have been out of breath a few times, but her vocal never wobbled. Impressively, she fit fragments of six songs into the five-minute medley, and at the end, surrounded by her dancers, dispatched a 'Mwah!' It was accompanied by a raised eyebrow and a smile that could only be described as cocky, as if she were thinking, 'Not bad, right?' The dancers' faces were damp with exertion, but Dua hadn't even broken a sweat. It might have been the stage make-up, but her face was noticeably dry, contributing to the impression that she was created from some kind of queenly essence available only to stars at the top of their game.

Her dancing deserves a chapter in its own right, insofar as it has generated hundreds of jokes and memes online. Suffice to say that it's not her strongest suit, when judged by the standard set by peers like Grande and Beyoncé. By the time of her Brits performance, she'd greatly improved, especially in the kind of formation-style choreography that keeps pop gigs and videos moving briskly along. But getting to that point had been a slog. Lipa was a singer. Dancing wasn't one of her core skills. There was a reason for that: singing occupied all her energy when she was on stage, and dancing required reserves of stamina she didn't yet have. Complex choreography demands so much physical power that some big names choose to mime their vocals in order to concentrate on dancing. But due to online mockery, she felt pushed to acquire the skill.

The way she moved on stage had been the subject of much ribbing since 2018, when two separate performances went viral. The first was at the Brit Awards in February. Nominated in five categories, she won British Breakthrough Act and British Female Solo Artist, and while she was there she sang 'New Rules'. Accompanied by several dozen backing dancers, she languidly made her way around the stage – gliding along a catwalk, pirouetting, gently lifting one leg, then the other – while singing live. It wasn't a breathtaking display, but it got the job done, and the whole thing would have passed without incident if she hadn't put a video of it on YouTube. It was spotted by a wag who left this comment: 'I love her lack of energy, go girl, give us nothing!'

That comment was endlessly tweeted and memed and even

became a catchphrase used when other pop stars, Selena Gomez and Jennie Kim of Blackpink among them, were considered to be slacking. But online japesters got even more mileage from a second Lipa performance, in Philadelphia in December 2018. This time, booked to play just four songs at local station Q102's Jingle Ball, she arrived with two backing dancers rather than the usual troupe, and the fact that it wasn't 'her' show might have contributed to her lack of oomph. Opening with 'One Kiss', she did some elementary steps, a few gentle Pilates-style stretches and twisted her hips from side to side.

It was the hip movement that fired up the critics. It was a regular part of her routine and had been labelled 'the pencil sharpener' — aptly, as the rotations resembled nothing so much as the lower half of her body being fed into a sharpener, with no variation in the movement. A fifteen-second clip of the dance at a show in 2017 became a meme, but it wasn't until the Q102 appearance that Lipa's onstage hip action really became a talking point. Filmed by someone in the audience and uploaded to YouTube, it drew thousands of pointed comments — some good-natured, some less so. She had refined the pencil sharpener into a side-to-side swish of her hips — it was now a relaxed sway that required little in the way of coordination or muscle power. Coupled with this was an abstracted gaze — as if she were thinking of something else throughout the song.

Viewer reaction ranged from, 'Can I talk to her production team?' to 'She is not ready to dance yet. And that outfit [a sequined green miniskirt and black bustier], she needs a better outfit ...'

to 'This was one of those radio/industry events and the stage is often cramped and the backgrounds unable to accommodate the visuals that normally go with the act.' One person compared her moves to someone trying to slip on a pair of shoes without using their hands. The most replayed moment of the nineteen-minute clip (which also included 'Blow Your Mind', 'IDGAF' and 'New Rules') was Lipa raising her leg high to (nearly) karate-kick one of the dancers during 'IDGAF'. Perhaps it was most-replayed because fans liked the aggression of the kick in a song about yet another hopeless ex, but it could also be that Lipa making a big physical effort during her stage routine simply fuelled further laughter.

Lipa was fully aware of the mostly good-natured scoffing. She read the comments and even mentioned the 'shoes' jibe a couple of years later on *The Tonight Show* in March 2022. By then, she was able to look back at that period and laugh, but in 2018 she took it to heart and was hurt.

Suddenly she was forced to give serious consideration to the part that dancing played in her performances. To be criticized for anything performance-related stung; the effort she put into all aspects of touring and TV work was colossal, from rehearsals to setlists. She could tolerate criticism if it related to an area where she'd tried her best and didn't quite reach the standard she'd set for herself, but to be slated for something she hadn't been able to master because she'd spread herself too thinly — that was unfair. Her explanation to *Vanity Fair* was that she'd tried 'to do everything at once' and hadn't had a chance to properly nail the dancing.

On a deeper level, she took the jokes and memes as a dig at

the career she'd built up. That probably wasn't the way they were intended: the viral 'Give us nothing!' comment and the video of her dancing at the Q102 show were spur-of-the-moment fan reactions and realistically meant little, but they made Lipa reflect that the onus was on her to prove herself – still. By definition, pop stardom is a transient occupation, and in 2018 Lipa only had one album to her name. That wasn't enough to prove anything, other than that she'd had a successful LP and an excellent run of hit singles. The proof would be in the second album, still two years away.

The singer always tries to go one better – she joked about it herself when she posted a dentist's X-ray of her mouth, which revealed she had one more tooth than the average adult. 'Your girl's been blessed with thirty-three teeth. I've always been an overachiever,' she tweeted. She's immensely demanding of herself; when she has time off recording and touring, she edits the Service95 weekly newsletter or produces an episode of her podcast or acts in her first movie.

The film is *Argylle*, a thriller about 'the world's greatest spy'; Lipa has a 'blonde bombshell' role, said *Page Six*, and also sings the theme tune. Filmed in 2021, it is set to premiere on Apple TV+ in 2023, but no other information has been released, other than that the producers hope to build it into a Bond-like franchise. Before *Argylle* even hit screens, Lipa was rumoured to be working on her second film, *Barbie*. The *Sun* claimed that she was offered the part, which is said to be a more prominent character than the one she plays in *Argylle*, because 'word spread around Hollywood' that she was on the way up. However, her participation hasn't been confirmed and other reports speculate that if she is involved, it could be in the form of singing on the soundtrack. There's been much excitement in the film industry about *Barbie*, which stars a phalanx of big names, such as Margot Robbie and Ryan Gosling, and is set to open in July 2023. The advance hype ensures millions of dollars at the box office, and potentially millions of eyes on Lipa. Quoting an insider, the *Sun* said this would be her film breakthrough and the start of an 'exciting future'. If true, it's another example of Lipa taking on a challenge in an area where she is inexperienced and acing it. Natural ability plays its part, but so does natural industriousness – Lipa offers a lesson in the power of quiet persistence and hard work.

Thus, being disparaged for her dancing was akin to a chink being found in her armour, through which self-doubt flowed. The triumph of winning two Brit Awards in 2018 was almost overshadowed by 'Give us nothing!' – in her eyes, she was found to be not good enough. For a while, she worried whenever she was filmed at a show, assuming punters were doing it not to have a keepsake of the gig but to laugh at her dancing. '[People would see] a video of me dancing and they're like, "Ah, well, she has no stage presence,"' she said in an interview with *Attitude* magazine. Her mental health was affected, and she took a break from Twitter.

Eventually, she would see the 'bullying', as she called it, as an incentive to improve: it made her 'want to dance my ass off ... and made me want to get better', she said in a 2021 Instagram post. Her super-charged 2021 Brits medley, three years after the contentious Brits performance, was a fantastic two-finger salute to those who had heckled, bullied or otherwise made her doubt herself.

Between 2018 and 2021, she applied the same tenacity she always did when set on accomplishing something difficult. She set about improving her stamina, the lack of which had spawned so much internet hilarity. The Q102 show in particular had made it plain that she found dancing – even the low-effort sort – tiring. Other videos from Dua's early career reveal the same listless movements, which worked the lower half of her body while her arms sometimes dangled at her sides.

To redress this, Lipa became a yoga devotee, which aided both her flexibility and her endurance. Her breath control improved and her core strengthened. (Core strength is key – when Madonna fell off the stage at the 2015 Brit Awards, she attributed her instant recovery to a supportive core.) She learned dance from Charm La'donna, choreographer to Selena Gomez, Kendrick Lamar and Rosalía, and practised to the point that she was almost unrecognizable by the time the Future Nostalgia tour finally got underway. The FN stage show was highly choreographed and divided into four demandingly physical segments, allowing Lipa to show the skills she'd picked up: she could now tango and swing and had the athleticism to pole-dance.

As she got fitter, she lost weight. It's unlikely that it was deliberate; Lipa is a strong advocate for body positivity, and it should be remembered that when her former modelling agency suggested she slim down, she left the industry rather than change herself in a way that seemed unnecessary to her. Moreover, she's a fan of good cooking. Interviews with her are full of sidenotes about her love of barbecues and roast dinners, and, given the chance, she'll recommend her favourite places. Or she'll cook right there in front of you: in August 2022, she prepared, roasted and carved a chicken in a video for the 'Summer Series' strand of her *At Your Service* podcast. 'I find the easiest way to cut the chicken is going for the breast first, then you get a really nice bit of the skin,' she offered, wielding the carving knife with practised ease. Her ex-partner, chef Isaac Carew, has also confirmed that she knows her way around the kitchen.

As a celebrity with an appetite and a sense of the ridiculous, she's been invited to eat in front of the cameras. Some online shows are entirely based around that simple premise: a famous person comes into the studio and eats. The highly popular American YouTube show *Hot Ones* from First We Feast has refined the concept: guests sample chicken wings drizzled with increasingly fiery hot sauces, eventually reaching a sauce with a Scoville heat rating of 2 million. (Between sauces, they discuss the star's career and latest projects.) It's a task that would fell many, but Lipa sailed through. It was only when she reached the seventh sauce (of ten) that she registered any heat. 'I feel like I'm sweating under my eyes,' she said mildly – a reserved, British response to a situation that has reduced other guests, such as Lizzo and Billie Eilish, to gasping and downing pints of water.

Similarly, in February 2022 while in Nashville on the Future Nostalgia tour, she posted a video of herself trying a local speciality: Nashville hot chicken. It's hard not to be impressed as she appreciatively digs into the extra spicy Damn Hot variety, then the even more daunting Shut the Cluck Up. The latter is made with Carolina Reaper chilli and described as the world's hottest chicken sandwich — YouTube is full of people filming themselves trying to eat one. Lipa's own experience with Shut the Cluck Up was that it failed to bring on anything close to a sweat. After fastidiously removing the pickle slices impaled on top of the chicken, she bit into each variety. Damn Hot was 'spicy, but not that spicy', and Shut the Cluck Up actually provoked a shrug: 'It's like a dry spice.'

But then, it would take an unimaginably virulent spice combination to induce a reaction — Lipa has revealed that when she has pizza, she drenches it in Scotch bonnet sauce and relishes every bite. She was brought up on the hottest Balkan food, and from childhood ate jars of avjar, a spicy pepper spread applied to everything from eggs to toast. It's the Albanian dish that, in her opinion, everyone has to try, but she also recommends a spinach-and-feta pie called *byrek me spinaq* and *sudzuk*, a spiced sausage sold in Eastern European groceries in the UK.

This is clearly a woman who likes her food. Though the rigours of touring call for a healthy diet, she still eats what she loves, in moderation. She's now equal to the demands of a complex, very physical show. And she's determined to stay that way — the Future Nostalgia tour retained the services of a health and nutrition coach, the kind of add-on that becomes necessary when you're playing ninety-one shows over ten months. The transformation started out as a response to being told she couldn't dance, but it came to encompass other aspects of her life. She's been delving into spirituality and has started to see a 'cosmic element' – her term – in her life as a performer. Lipa isn't the first musician to have described her job as a mission to help bring people together, but she's sincere in her belief that her songs can help people feel 'seen or understood', she told *Vogue* in 2022.

The conversation with Vogue took place in March, during the first (American) leg of Future Nostalgia, when she was reacquainting herself with playing in front of live audiences. Those US dates, which kicked off in Miami on 9 February, were a very big deal. Finally, she could play songs from her second album and see people react right in front of her. Amassing billions of streams and a string of hit tracks was great in terms of monument-building, but it was only when Lipa saw her 'Loves' – the name adopted by her superfans – wigging out in the flesh that she was able to admit to herself that, yes, she had made a record that would be remembered as one of the twenty-first-century's great pop albums. If she glanced at the books every night, she would have also seen that ticket sales usually amounted to well over $1 million a show.

She could also reflect on how far she had come since 'Give us nothing!' There was some vestigial bitterness about the trolling she'd endured on social media, and she still felt that she'd been an easy, unfair target. Unlike pop stars who had 'trained' for the job by coming through the Disney or Nickelodeon channels – these include Ariana Grande, Miley Cyrus, Selena Gomez and Demi Lovato, who starred in tween sitcoms like *Hannah Montana* and *Sam & Cat* before switching to music – she'd had no grounding in showbiz. Once Grande and the rest transitioned to full-time singing, they were able to slough off the perkiness of their TV roles and be themselves, but those years in the kids' TV system had provided the tools for furthering their careers, including dancing skills. There was simply never a time in, for example, Grande's pop career when she couldn't walk onto a stage and pull off rapid-fire choreography. Cyrus, too, could acquit herself admirably, thanks to *Hannah Montana* storylines, such as one that had her throwing shapes at a Western hoedown.

Lipa calls such training 'pop-star camp'. She didn't name any pop stars, nor specify what 'camp' they'd attended — an ardent feminist and supporter of other women, she wouldn't judge anyone who'd been professionally instructed. The thrust is that she feels *she* was judged, by fans, for not having a complete pop-star skillset.

Still, dance-revenge was hers, and in a joyous way. First, in January 2021, she appeared in a video for British *Vogue*'s lockdown 'home-school series', Vogue U. Her episode was called 'Let Dua Lipa Teach You How to Dance'. In the hilarious preamble, she said she'd always been a natural on the dance floor and was constantly besieged by fans asking how they could match her brilliance. 'You almost certainly can't,' she said — but she would try to help them along. 'Pirouette! Don't be lazy!' she bawled at a group of dancers as they gamely tried to learn her moves. 'Attitude!' Then it was time for the 'stage presence' segment ...

All the supposed weak points in her performances were sent up in the three-minute video, and she emerged the victor. Some viewers didn't realize it was a comedy sketch and were agog at the progress she'd made — it wasn't so long ago that she'd been laughed at, and now here she was, teaching professional dancers how to dance. Most got the joke, though, and she went up even further in their estimation. It is, after all, incredibly hard to source an artist who sings, dances, looks great *and* has the acting chops to make nearly 800,000 viewers laugh. 'Go, girl, give us everything,' a fan wrote, capturing in five words the change she had achieved.

Once the Future Nostalgia tour was on the road, she continued to clap back. There was a guest slot on Jimmy Fallon's *Tonight Show* in March 2022, three days after she'd played a sold-out Madison Square Garden (15,461 seats filled, $2.05 million taken at the box office). Fallon was an old pal, or at least enough of one to tell her, 'I love you, bud,' as she sat on his sofa. She chuckled at his effusiveness, but he meant it — back in April 2020, the green screen she set up to enhance her Zoomed-in performance provided a show 'when we didn't have a show'. Finally face-to-face again, he reminded her of it, and because it was two years on Lipa was able to reveal that she hadn't been keen on creating a green screen in the first place. Having to learn the skill was daunting — 'scary', in fact — but once she'd done it, she was delighted to have pulled it off.

Fallon congratulated her on the highly positive reviews the tour was attracting: 'They love the dancing, and on social media they're loving one dance in particular.' At his last four words, she laughed, knowing what was coming. She was OK with it now, she assured him. She'd made it through the self-doubt and come out the other side. What had been a confidence-eroding experience in 2018 was something she now saw as a positive. She actually remembered the mockery 'with such fondness', she told him, because the bullying had forced her to grow into the performer she wanted to be. More than most pop stars, Lipa excels at learning: if the old way doesn't work any more, learn a new way.

So, she'd incorporated – yes – the 'viral dance' into her 2022 stage show. She was now so sure of her dancing that the 'pencil sharpener' had become a benign memory. To pay tribute to it at her gigs, she did the pencil sharpener in the encore, 'Don't Start Now' – and it was wondrous. Standing on a platform with her dancers arrayed on either side, she opened the song with the instantly familiar slow-motion hip flexes, followed by a languid segue into low-energy leg stretches. The audience reaction was loud and joyous. Now unshakeable in her choreography – this isn't to say she could outdance Beyoncé or Bruno Mars, but she was good – she was having fun, renewing the bond between herself and her fans.

Naturally, Fallon wanted to see the dance for himself, even offering to do it with her. What could she do but oblige? Standing side by side in front of his desk with right feet extended and Dua shouting, 'Hip, hip, hip, hip!' the pair twisted their hips in time. 'That almost hurt me,' Fallon said bravely after he'd returned to his chair. She later told Fallon that she's had 'a lot of "pinch me" moments' in her career. This had to be one of them.

Chapter 15

WORK HARD AND BE NICE

'I think that there are three Dua Lipas in the world, and none of them is ever not working.' That was a tweet from a fan, read out by Kimmy B, a presenter on the Miami radio station Hits 97.3. It was 11 June 2018, and she and Lipa were on stage in front of a live audience at a Q&A session arranged to tie in with her show at the Bayfront Park Amphitheatre the following night. She'd played the Bonnaroo Festival in Manchester, Tennessee, the night before and got a flight at four in the morning to make the 800-mile journey to Miami.

'There's only one of me,' Lipa laughed. 'The exciting part of my job is that I get to go to a different place every single day and I never do the same thing twice.' But when that's your schedule literally *every* day, does it lose its lustre? As Kimmy pointed out, she had been on a frenetic treadmill since 'Be the One' came out in December 2016, and it hadn't stopped. But Lipa was firm in her view that working as much as possible was worth it. It brought her into contact with new fans, and the love they lavished on her was like nothing else. She abides by two rules, she once told another interviewer: 'Work hard and be nice.' She's so emphatic about the rules that there's now a GIF that shows her at an interview with the caption, 'Work hard and be nice. Always.' Along the same gently jokey lines, *Heat* magazine once tagged her as 'one of the hardest working ladies in pop, only in the news for winning awards and being fantastic'. That was nothing more than the truth.

A huge appetite for grafting was instilled in early childhood, when her father told her: 'You have to work really, really hard, just to have a tiny bit of luck.' To put it another way: there's no such thing as 'luck' – you get lucky by creating it yourself. Her ambitious parents were her example; she couldn't remember a time when they weren't working multiple jobs and going to university in the evening. They adapted to every situation they found themselves in. It's a quality Dua inherited that has come in handy when she finds herself in a situation that demands change, such as the need, after the 'viral dance' trolling, to substantially raise her choreography game.

What really rammed it home was moving back to London at fifteen and finding out that the onus was on her to look after herself. Having to do her own laundry and cook meals was, for her, a huge responsibility, and it altered her view of life. She has repeatedly mentioned the shock of having to become her own cleaner and cook, and still talks about it to this day – it's part of her narrative because it affected how she manages her career. 'I know that no one's going to go out and get it for me,' she said. 'I have to work really hard in order to do it myself.' There's something poignant about her conviction that nobody would be prepared to help her, but it did implant a form of self-reliance that hasn't let her down yet. And she's admitted that when she has time off, she spends much of it in bed, so she does take time to recharge.

Naturally, she's also on top of the substructure of her career. Companies House, the government body that keeps track of limited and limited-liability companies in the UK, featured her in a blogpost in 2018. It commented approvingly on her having registered her company, Dua Lipa Limited, early – it was incorporated in July 2014, shortly after she signed with Warner Bros., and the nature of the business is 'artistic creation'. She's listed as the sole director. (For reasons that are unclear, her first four singles – 'New Love', 'Be the One', 'Last Dance' and 'Hotter than Hell' – were released on her own 'label', Dua Lipa Limited, rather than on Warner Bros.) Urging other businesses to register with Companies House, the blogpost used Lipa as an example of why it's important. 'Dua Lipa Limited is separate from Dua Lipa the owner. If the company loses money, it will not have to come out of the pocket of Dua Lipa herself. Registering her company with us also means the name is protected by law.'

That's the 'work hard' rule. Then there's the 'being nice' part, which is as important as putting in the hours. 'Niceness' boils down to approaching commitments with a positive attitude, but it's much harder than it sounds, and here's why.

Until recently, there was little sign of the music industry having a duty of care toward artists. The conventional view was that people were desperate to make it in music, so why should the industry be responsible for their wellbeing? They knew what they were getting into: punishingly long days were and still are the norm. Catching a flight in the middle of the night so a musician can do a day of promo 800 miles away is par for the course. Commonly, that promo day will be followed by a show in the evening and a meet-and-greet (occasionally known as a shake-and-fake) afterward.

Artists are becoming more vocal about the effects of overwork — the rapidly rising singers Arlo Parks and Sam Fender cancelled tours in 2022 because it was affecting their mental health. Parks, who won the 2021 Mercury Music Prize and a Brit Award for Breakthrough Artist in the same year, said, 'I've been on the road on and off for the last eighteen months, filling every spare second in between and working myself to the bone.'

Lipa does exactly that. She told *WSJ. Magazine* that she's motivated not only by an ingrained need to excel but also by the underlying worry that 'the rug could be pulled out from under my feet if I don't work hard enough'. No matter how many billions of Spotify streams or millions of pounds she amasses, that feeling never quite disappears, and she pushes herself to make sure the rug stays where it is.

She's been in the business longer than Parks and has learned to pace herself, making the burden less onerous, but the desire to work is what gets her out of bed every morning. This is the girl who retook her A Levels just for the challenge, and launched a commitment-heavy weekly newsletter and podcast as she was about to set off on a world tour. But along with the appetite for toil is the pledge to 'be nice'. It comes down to a pressing desire to make things as pleasant as possible for all concerned, knowing that it will reap rewards. Her private feelings about eighteen-hour days packed with promotion are unknown, but in public Lipa gives the impression that she's delighted to be talking to the eighth journalist of the day. It's an unspoken truth in the music business that artists are, at best, ambivalent about the endless rounds of face-to-face interviews, breakfast-show appearances and phone chats with interviewers on the other side of the world, and many don't hide their feelings. Not Lipa: she's smiling, friendly, approachable—the dream interviewee.

What's remarkable is her patience as she answers the same questions she's been asked since 2016, which always include: you moved to London alone when you were just fifteen? How did you get started in music? Is there a rivalry between you and other female singers? Whatever she's thinking, she always treats the questions, and the interviewers, as if they're important. That also applies to more nuanced questions, such as one posed by a culture-and-lifestyle journalist in 2021: does she benefit from 'pretty privilege'? It was a jibe disguised as a query: is her success attributable to her good looks, rather than a decade of solid graft? Though taken aback, Lipa was courteous, saying she takes care of herself because she feels better when she does. Later, she told the interviewer – still politely, without rancour – that she was confident she had done well because of her talent and drive rather than her looks. She added that the question had been weighing on her mind since the interviewer had asked. The latter was startled into silence. The article ended with the writer proffering a sincere apology to Lipa. A win, there, for Lipa and for niceness.

When the media try to unearth negative stories about her, the pickings are pretty slim. One gossip site tried its best in 2022, with a video called 'Celebrities Who Tried to Warn Us About Dua Lipa'. The best it could come up with was that at the 2019 Brit Awards, Lipa – who'd been nominated for Best Single and Best Video – closed the door to her dressing room and removed her name from the door. The video framed it as if she were rudely avoiding fraternizing with the other artists milling around backstage. Calvin Harris, one of the celebrities who ostensibly 'tried to warn us', was depicted as the nice guy because he left his door ajar, welcoming all comers.

What the video didn't mention was that later in the evening Lipa was to perform a live version of 'One Kiss' with Harris, including fiddly choreography, and was more than likely not up to socializing before going on stage. Her dressing room was also in the most visible spot backstage, next to a beauty spa, and none of the many stars who visited the spa before the show began could resist popping their heads in to say hello to Lipa. Thus, the closed door. ('One Kiss' took the Best Single gong. In the same category, she was also nominated for 'IDGAF', and both singles received

Best Video nominations. It's rare to have two nods in the same section.)

The same video claimed that Taylor Swift also tried to warn the world. It seemed that during the decade-long 'feud' between Swift and Kanye West that began when West barged on stage while Swift was accepting an MTV VMA Award in 2009, Lipa had once expressed a preference for West's music over Swift's. She's a hardcore hip-hop aficionado, so when she was asked who she liked more as an artist, West was the automatic choice. Swift fans felt let down because Lipa had once been pictured wearing a Taylor *Speak Now* T-shirt (Swift saw the photo and tweeted, 'I am SCREECHING WITH JOY'); preferring West's music was tantamount to treason. Lipa received scores of tweets with 'snake' emojis, and there was even a death threat. Asked to explain herself on American TV, she said she hadn't been picking sides; she had no interest in their quarrel — and that seemed to quell the uprising. From Swift herself, there was no comment. Far from warning us about Dua, the American singer rose above it, and the last word on the matter came from Lipa in a 2018 interview with *Wired*: 'I love Taylor. We've met a couple of times. She's amazing, what an incredible artist.'

The upshot is that when Lipa counsels others to be nice, she's prepared to lead by example. 'Work hard and be nice' isn't an empty catchphrase but words she lives by.

Chapter 16

A FEMALE ALPHA

In a message to her 10 million Twitter followers in November 2022, Lipa marvelled that she had just sung 'Cold Heart' with Elton John at Dodger Stadium in Los Angeles. At the start of her career, she wrote, she couldn't have envisaged being part of an event like this—the final American show of John's long-running Farewell Yellow Brick Road tour, during which she appeared for the encore. That night, 20 November, was the 269th of 333 dates, with the finale set for 8 July 2023 in Stockholm. By the time it finishes, it will be the third highest-grossing tour in history. Dua was elegant in the mode of a 1950s jazz singer, in a floor-length black one-shouldered dress with a 15ft train and full-length gloves. Elton, for his part, was Peak Elton: long, sequined Dodgers bathrobe and matching baseball cap. Some 50,000 people greeted her as she glided out of the wings — there was no one there who didn't know her name.

It was a doubly special occasion for both, because on the same night 'Cold Heart' won the Best Collaboration category at the American Music Awards. The next day, Dua tweeted to the @eltonofficial Twitter account that it had been 'an honour, a privilege and a joy' to sing with him.

A few hours later, she tweeted again. Two words: 'JONI MITCHELL!!!!!!!!' Below was a picture taken backstage at the stadium: Lipa and the great songwriter sitting together, Mitchell in an armchair and Lipa perched on an arm, with her right arm draped around Mitchell's shoulders. Mitchell, who turned seventy-nine two weeks before, is smiling radiantly, and she's marvellous in her own right, but what makes the picture special is Dua's joy and humility at meeting a giant among artists. Her head is resting on Joni's, her eyes are closed and her smile semaphores amazement and joy. In this photo, one of the biggest pop stars to emerge from Britain in the past decade is the super-fan. It also says something about her understanding of how popular music developed and her reverence for forebears such as Mitchell and John.

A week later, posting on Instagram from a recording studio, she offered up another talking point. It was a Polaroid picture of Lipa sitting on a sofa, shoulder to shoulder with another smiling seventy-nine-year-old: Mick Jagger. 'Sweeet weeek,' read the caption. Their meeting was a source for conjecture. What were they doing there, the 'pop superstar' and the 'legendary rocker'? Media speculation offered three possibilities: Jagger was recording a duet for her third album; she was recording one for the next Rolling Stones LP, due out in 2023; or they had simply run into each other at a studio and grabbed a picture together. In the absence of clarification from Lipa, any of the guesses could be right. One paper added that the Gucci leather jacket she wore in the shot retailed at £33,000, inciting a wave of comments from readers shocked that she had spent so much money during the cost-of-living crisis. It's far more likely that the jacket was either a gift or sold to her at a hefty discount.

When she tweeted that once upon a time it would have been impossible to have pictured herself at the Elton gig, she was also sending a tacit message: at her core she was still the striver from north-west London, the schoolgirl who wished her name was Amber or Ella, the fifteen-year-old in Pristina who decided that her musical future was in London and persuaded her parents to let her move there. What's happened since then has been remarkable, but some part of her will always find it hard to believe she's been so 'lucky' — though luck, of course, played a smaller part than talent and indomitable commitment. As Dugi Lipa says, you have to work hard to get a little luck.

Dua sometimes ascribes her success to 'magic' or 'manifesting'. That's not magic as in potions and spells — her most recent single at the time of writing happens to be called 'Potion', but the potion in the song is a metaphor for late-night canoodling rather than anything supernatural. Lipa's idea of magic is more a belief that if she wishes for something fervently enough and works toward it, it will happen: 'manifesting', in other words. 'I needed to manifest a new positive energy in my life,' she has said, regarding a romantic relationship that no longer worked for her. She brought her brother and sister onto the stage at the 2018 Brit Awards so they would know that, as far as she was concerned, 'magic is real'.

Friend and frequent co-writer Sarah Hudson starts all Lipa's studio sessions with a tarot reading, which 'instantly changes the energy in the room', Lipa told *Song Exploder*. The readings open the door to frank conversation between Lipa, Hudson, Koz and any other writers and producers who happen to be on the session, and the conversations lead to songs being written. Manifesting and tarot cards help Lipa get hold of the deeper feelings that propel her music. Those feelings might end up enrobed in dazzling beats, effects and techy gloss, but they're at the heart of what she does. Dance-crying wouldn't have existed without Lipa laying her heart on the line.

She moved from the dance-crying of *Dua Lipa* to the disco escapism of *Future Nostalgia*, and Album Three, whenever it's ready, will take a different path again. Plans for the third record's release are still in the formative stages at this writing – she said in September 2022 that something 'might' materialize in the new year. That's if she feels 'really good about it' – few artists have a stronger sense of quality control. If the rollout is similar to *FN*'s, a single could appear in the second half of 2023, with the album following in 2024. That would be four years since *FN*, which is an aeon in pop terms and would have most managers and labels twitching with anxiety. Lipa's team, though, are confident that the wait will be worth it. They would have also been buoyed by the news that *Dua Lipa* passed 10 billion Spotify streams in September 2022 – the first album by a woman to reach that figure.

The demand is there, and it's unlikely to dissipate before the new record is ready. While fans wait, there could be, who knows, a live album (her Rio and Amsterdam shows were filmed, so it's a possibility). And even as she painstakingly constructs the new LP, nicknamed 'DL3', we know her phone is full of ideas for albums four and five. In the meantime, fans speculate about what direction 'DL3' will take. One site confidently predicts that it will be a rock album. Other guesses are EDM and hyperpop – or perhaps something funky in a Jamiroquai vein? Her parents played his records at home when Dua was a toddler, so it's not out of the question. Or how about disco à la *Future Nostalgia*, but with a moodier, late-night ambience along the lines of Britney Spears's *Blackout* LP? Anything is possible, with the (probable) exception of a straight-up glittery return to the *FN* style with nothing in the way of innovation – Lipa doesn't revisit previous sounds.

Stardom changes some people beyond recognition, but Lipa seems less mutable. She was a bright, attuned woman when she started out, and remains so today. Her interest in architecture, art and books hasn't diminished; if anything, it's been heightened by constant travel. Unusually for a major pop star in her twenties, she puts equal value on political activism and the froth of the fashion world – the Service95 newsletter and *At Your Service* podcast continue to reveal an enquiring mind and a desire to learn from her guests, who have included Mo Farah, Monica

Lewinsky and Yazidi human-rights campaigner Nadia Murad, who was accompanied by Amal Clooney. The *Guardian* believes that she's 'head and shoulders above most [celebrity podcasters], simply because she listens'.

All that's changed since the early days is the opportunities that now come her way. They're many and varied, and often surprising, resulting in a career timeline unlike that of any other big pop name. She models for Versace but was also invited to give a speech at the 2022 Booker Prize ceremony about her love of reading. She's the 'face' (perhaps 'nose' is more apt) of Yves Saint Laurent's Libre perfume but also discussed the music industry's gender pay gap at the Cambridge Union. Her first album has been streamed 10 billion times and many of her singles have clocked up over 1 billion apiece, but all those streams co-exist with receiving a leadership award from the Atlantic Council think tank. In November 2022, she was granted Albanian citizenship by President Bajram Begaj himself, but she also cheered on England in the World Cup (there had been baseless rumours that she would perform at the opening ceremony in Qatar, but as a longtime advocate for the LGBT+ community, she never had any intention of taking part because of the country's human-rights record, and especially its treatment of gay people).

On 28 November, the day after the citizenship ceremony, Lipa played the last show of the Future Nostalgia tour. The location was Skanderbeg Square in Albania's capital, Tirana. Estimated attendance was 200,000 – her largest audience as a headliner. Ten months and ninety-one concerts after the tour started in Miami, she was back in her ancestral Balkans. Her social media post showed her holding an Albanian flag, alongside which was the caption: 'So happy to be in Tirana, Albania, as the newest citizen to perform for you all tonight.'

Female alphas are not the new 'girlbosses' – that term, coined by entrepreneur Sophia Amoruso in her 2014 memoir #Girlboss, has been discredited because it became synonymous with privileged white businesswomen who failed to empower women below them. (Coincidentally, Lipa's sister, Rina, once modelled for Nasty Gal, the highly popular fashion line formerly owned by Amoruso.) Lipa's female alpha is more realistic. It doesn't demand supremacy over men or losing touch with one's vulnerability – rather, it applauds empathy and kindness while refusing to be subjugated by men, whether it's one of Lipa's no-hoper exes, a boss or a politician.

From childhood on, her idols have been the grande femmes of pop: Madonna, Alicia Keys, P!nk, Nelly Furtado. Observing and following them helped her find her own path in the music business, and one of her dreams is to provide similar inspiration to the next pop generation. Another desire is that women will work hand-in-hand with each other and with men, striving for an end to racism, gender inequity, ableism and homophobia.

Asked whether she gets bored with constantly singing the same songs, she said, 'It's not really about me, it's about the listeners.' She views her career as an alliance between herself and the fans – another difference between her and most other artists at her level. She named her podcast At Your Service for a reason: it's not about her, it's about her and us. That's a pretty good way to be going on.

PICTURE CREDITS

INDEX

Good Morning Britain (GMB) 39
Good Pop, Bad Pop (Cocker) 50
Gosling, Jake 54, 57
Gosling, Ryan 224
Goulding, Ellie 198
GQ 79, 160
Grammy Awards 40, 97, 109, 144–5, 154, 183, 202, 207, 216
Grand, Lisa 217–18
Grande, Ariana 62, 145, 189, 190, 195, 207, 216, 228
Grazia 84
Grimes, Chelcee 62
Grohl, Dave 215
Guardian 68, 83, 89, 92, 94, 131, 136, 150, 160, 164, 171–4, 177, 201, 204, 246
Guetta, David 135

Hadid, Anwar 67–9, 68, 161–3
Hadid, Bella 67
Hadid, Gigi 67
Halliwell, Geri 46
'Hallucinate' 14, 164, 169, 208, 213
Halsey, Raye and Sigrid 83
Hannah Montana 228, 229
Harlow, Jack 67, 158
Harper's Bazaar 43, 142
Harris, Calvin 8, 96, 102–6, 149, 166, 189, 198, 238
Harry, Debbie 145
Haynie, Emile 70
health and wellbeing 124, 143, 224–8, 236
Heat 9, 90, 234
Hemsworth, Liam 206
'High' 106, 210–11
Hits 97.3 61, 233
'Hollaback Girl' 213
'Homesick' 77, 78, 93–4, 100, 199–201
Hot Ones 148, 226
'Hotter than Hell' 58–65, 69, 71, 76–7, 86, 89, 160, 162–3, 235
Houston, Whitney 145
Howell-Baptiste, Kirby 39
Hozier 20
Hudson, Sarah 49, 69, 117–20, 193, 244

'I Don't Give a Fuck', *see* 'IDGAF'
i newspaper 179
'I'd Rather Go Blind' 47, 211, 217
'IDGAF' 8, 72, 91, 95–103, 160, 222, 238

Idolator 204, 210
'If Only' 195
Independent 128, 192
Influencer Intelligence 87
Insta-stream 181–2
Instagram 14, 22, 23, 44, 68, 84, 90, 111, 113, 133, 151, 158, 161, 167, 180–82, 193, 224, 242
INXS 163
ITV 54

Jagger, Bianca 181
Jagger, Mick 242–3
James, Etta 47, 211, 217
James, Greg 57
Jamiroquai 147, 168, 245
Jessie J 48, 49, 190, 215
Jimmy Kimmel Live! 91
Jingle Ball (Q102) 221
Jingle Bell Ball (Capital FM) 104
John Peel Stage 88
John, Sir Elton 120, 179, 180–81, 190–92, 241–3
Johnson, Boris 11, 99, 161

KAMP-FM 189
Kardashian, Kim 145
Kentish, Joe 24–5, 62–5, 118, 120–21, 128
Keys, Alicia 29, 33, 247
Kid Cudi 192–3
Killing Eve 39
Kim, Jennie 221
Kim, Nelly, *see* Furtado, Nelly
Kimmel, Jimmy 91
Kimmy B 233
Kirk, Jonathan 166–7
Kirkpatrick, Ian 125, 159
'Kiss and Make Up' 62, 196
Kiss FM 104
Kitchen Disco 168
Klein, Paul 67
KOKO 50
Kosovo 17–22, 28–34, 37, 44–5, 64, 134, 147–56, 184
'Kosovo's Got Talent' school talent show 29
Kozmeniuk, Stephen ('Koz') 70–73, 76, 117, 119–20, 193

La Bodega Negra 45, 61, 68